Bill Shepard traveled extensively around Northern California, into the rugged Sierra Nevada Mountains, and up along the coast. Join him on a journey through California's past, when only the hardiest, the luckiest or the most stubborn survived.

California CORNERSTONE

BY BILL SHEPARD

(as reprinted from the pages of the
Woodland Daily Democrat)

SHEPARDSON
BOOKS

CALIFORNIA CORNERSTONE

Published by Shepardson Books
A division of Stark House Press
1315 H Street
Eureka, CA 95501, USA
griffinskye3@sbcglobal.net
www.starkhousepress.com

"California Cornerstone" originally published as a weekly column and copyright © 1963, 1964 by *The Daily Democrat* of Woodland, CA. Reprinted with permission of *The Daily Democrat*.

"A Good Friend Remembered" copyright © 2012 by Darrell Dodds

"The Camping Cornerstone" copyright © 2012 by Greg Shepard

All rights reserved

ISBN: 1-933586-57-5
ISBN-13: 978-1-933586-57-1

Text set in Kennerley Old Style
Cover design and layout by Mark Shepard, www.SHEPGRAPHICS.COM
Proofreading by Rick Ollerman

PUBLISHER'S NOTE
Without limiting the rights under copyright reserved above, no part of this publication may be reproduced, stored, or introduced into a retrieval system or transmitted in any form or by any means (electronic, mechanical, photocopying, recording or otherwise) without the prior written permission of both the copyright owner and the above publisher of the book.

First Shepardson Books Edition: September 2012

Reprint Edition

California
CORNERSTONE

A GOOD FRIEND AND MENTOR REMEMBERED BY DARRELL DODDS

When I heard of Bill's passing last March, a flood of emotions washed over me triggering memories of both joy and sadness. Those of us of a certain age become used to hearing of former friends and colleagues dying but Bill was one of those good, kind, honest and generous men that we hope will find a way to defy the fate of lesser mortals.

Shortly after Bill's death, I was asked to write a brief obituary for the American Horse Publications and the Livestock Publications Council, two groups that were profoundly affected by Bill's contributions over the years. It was perhaps the easiest and hardest thing I've ever had to write, in part, because my thoughts kept straying back to the early 1980s in Quincy, California, where we shared campfires in the Plumas National Forest backcountry as well as many sleepless nights trying to figure out a way to save my little community newspaper from bankruptcy.

Recently Greg Shepard informed me he was publishing a collection of Bill's writings written while Bill was a reporter for the *Woodland Daily Democrat* in the early 1960s. To be honest, although I knew Bill well, I'd never read any of his early work and don't remember discussing any of his previous jobs or career changes with him. Bill lived in the moment more than any man I ever knew so I guess I should not be surprised by the fact that he didn't discuss work that he enjoyed, completed, and moved on from.

Looking back, I was always impressed by Bill's knowledge of the California Goldrush, a topic that came up frequently when we were hiking through some of the country that had been most affected, for better and for worse, by hordes of ill-equipped miners seeking their fortune. I realize now that Bill's knowledge came from relentless research into California's history that only a young, highly energetic Midwestern journalism student could bring to the topic. Please take the time to savor Bill's storytelling on the following pages. You'll not only gain knowledge about some of California's earliest characters, you'll also learn more about the author himself.

I met Bill in 1977 when I was selling advertising for Feather Publishing Company, a family-owned regional newspaper chain headquartered in Quincy, California, a small mountain community north of Lake Tahoe. Bill's wife, Joanne, worked as a typesetter for the *Feather River Bulletin* and through her I met Bill, who was publishing a small tabloid at the time called the *California Camper*.

Bill ran this little business venture out of his and Joanne's modest two-story log cabin, giving him the opportunity to do the things he loved to do the most: write, photograph and backpack the length and breadth of the Sierra Nevada mountains.

In 1978, I quit my job with Feather Publishing and started my own weekly newspaper called the *Green Mountain Gazette*. As my business grew, I soon realized I needed a tight-fisted businessman who could keep expenses from spinning out of control. Bill, who had a reputation for stretching a dollar, volunteered to help on a part-time basis and soon assumed the duties of business manager, accountant, copy editor, darkroom technician and all-around handyman.

During the summer of 1980, the previous year's energy crisis took its toll on California's recreational areas, and with far fewer tourists passing through, advertising dollars dried up. So did *California Camper*. Although he hated to leave his beloved mountains, Bill and Joanne moved to Sacramento where Bill took over management of the *California Horse Review*, a hugely successful all-breed publication that had benefited from the explosive popularity of the recreational horse industry in the 1950s, '60s and '70s.

Although Bill never had a passion for horses, he did like publishing a quality product and his influence was felt immediately as the magazine's content and design took on a decidedly more modern appearance.

In 1982, the same forces that shut down Bill's little tabloid doomed my own publishing venture. When Bill heard the news that we had stopped the presses at *Green Mountain Gazette*, he called and offered a freelance assignment covering the 1982 Snaffle Bit Futurity in Reno, along with a couple of other freelance writers, noted equine journalists Betsy Lynch and Jenny Meyer.

While working at the Snaffle Bit Futurity, Bill told me about a help-wanted ad running in his magazine for an editor for the *Appaloosa News* in Moscow, Idaho. On a lark, I sent a letter expressing my interest. Several weeks later, I packed everything I owned into a 1981 Ford Econoline van and moved to Moscow, where I entered the equine publishing profession.

A few years later, I had the opportunity to return the favor. In the mid-1980s, *California Horse Review* had sold to a venture capitalist and Bill was looking for another opportunity. I'd heard about an opening at the *Paint Horse Journal* in Fort Worth and suggested he apply. Under Ed Roberts' guidance, the fledgling Paint Horse industry was beginning to bloom and the *Paint Horse Journal* needed an editor who could put out a professional magazine without going broke in the process. Bill was the right guy at the right time.

For the next few years, Bill and I had the opportunity to get together at AHP meetings or other industry functions to exchange information, a few good stories and a beer or two. Bill was always generous with his advice but never offered it unless asked. He took great delight in helping others launch their careers, and so assuming a leadership role with the Livestock Publications Council after retiring from the *Paint Horse Journal* in 1992 was a natural.

As luck would have it, I assumed Bill's position at APHA, where I remained for 10 years before moving on to *Horse & Rider* and now *Western Horseman*. I have no idea what I would be doing today had it not been for Bill's friendship and the serendipitous opportunities that he steered my way when I needed them most.

Although Bill was content to be a quiet, behind-the-scenes kind of guy, his influence in our industry was large and significant. He will be missed by all who knew him.

KRUM, TX
JUNE 2012

THE CAMPING CORNERSTONE
BY GREG SHEPARD

Everyone's childhood is just a little bit different. The Shepard kids spent theirs running around the neighborhood, riding bikes, catching butterflies, reading comics, playing games in the backyard and baseball in the park, mowing the lawn, singing songs around the piano—and camping. Dad loved to camp. Whether in a tent, with backpacks, with a trailer or just out of the back of our jeep, he loved to take his family camping, out into nature. We traveled all over Northern California in the 1960's—up to La Porte and into the mining country of Howland and Poker Flats; backpacking to Emigrant Basin north of Yosemite; through Grass Valley, up to Downieville and Shasta, over to Placerville in the Gold Country; all over the place. If there was a small historical town and an area you could only get to by jeep, my dad was there. And so were we.

I had no idea at the time that all these trips were providing inspiration to my dad for a series of weekly articles he would begin to write for the *Woodland Daily Democrat*. To us kids, the Sierra Nevadas were our extended playground. Growing up near Sacramento, in that flat, fertile Central Valley, you are always aware of the Coast Range on one side, and the Sierras on the other. Hard to get lost in a town like Woodland if you could see those two mountain ranges off in the distance. You always knew where west and east were.

When it came to camping, we usually headed east. Oh, there were the trips up the coast, to Dimmick State Park in the giant redwoods, to Patrick's Point on the foggy coast. But mostly I remember the trips into the hot, dry mountains that always loomed off in the distance. They must have been a beacon to my dad. I will never forget those trips to Poker Flat. You had to have a jeep with 4-wheel drive to get there, and it still took a fair amount of cautious driving. First we'd drive to La Porte, where they had a great general store that served the best cold soda pop you could want. We'd be so parched by the time we got there, all we could think about were those bottles of crème soda and grape and orange.

After resting a bit in La Porte, we'd start the climb to Howland Flat, not much more than a bunch of broken down building frames in the 1960's, but once a prosperous mining town. This was our last stop before winding down into the canyon where the old mining camp of Poker Flat once thrived. Once there, we ran around the boulders to catch lizards, fished for trout, and checked out the crumbling cliffs where the hydraulic hoses had blasted away half the mountain in search of gold less than a hundred years before.

My dad was a very patient father. He'd let us run loose to discover the treasures around us. I remember catching three small trout one summer, which I was so proud of—except that I didn't like to eat fish. But my dad cooked them right up and enjoyed the fruits of my labors himself, so nothing went to waste. This was where *California Cornerstone* was born.

California Cornerstone ran on the editorial page of the *Daily Democrat* from January 24, 1963 to July 30, 1964, starting out sporadically and eventually becoming a weekly column. These short articles covered mostly the era of the late 1800's, after gold had been discovered in the state. Each was a little story, tales of the miners and explorers, the early settlers and Native Americans, the movers and shakers and the common men, the bandits and liars, all the wild characters that made Northern California history so damn colorful, and so much fun to read about.

My dad wrote about what he knew and what he loved. He loved the mountains. And he loved history. I remember reading the column when I was a kid, about eleven to twelve years old, but the stories didn't have the impact that they do today. I took it all for granted. Now I hear my dad's gentle sense of humor, his love of story-telling (he relished telling those long jokes that took forever to reach their punchline but were always worth it when he got there); I hear his voice in these articles and I remember all those great camping trips, and I wouldn't trade that childhood for anything in the world.

EUREKA, CA
JUNE 2012

California
CORNERSTONE

FIREPROOFING

Throughout the Sierra Nevada gold mining region there are many stone and brick buildings still standing. Considering the amount of wood available as a building material, it is unusual to find so many stone structures. The first settlers, however, learned through bitter experience to choose a fireproof material.

Hardly a single major camp of the Sierra did not have one or more fires. In many cases, fire struck again and again until wooden buildings were replaced by those of stone.

Most of the early gold seekers spent little time in building a house. They first lived in brush tents and later in frame and canvas shelters which were an open invitation to disaster. Heating and cooking were generally by means of an open fire, adding to the fire hazard.

Commercial buildings were on a par with the miners' shelters. Canvas and wood were generally used in the construction of a camp store.

Since there was little flat room available for building in the majority of the Sierra Camps, houses and stores were crowded side by side into a small area. Once a fire started it usually wiped out an entire town.

Nevada City had major fires in 1851, 1856, and 1863. Sonora suffered severe fire losses in 1849, 1852 and 1853. Columbia was burned in 1854, 1857 and 1861, Grass Valley in 1857, Downieville in 1852, Placerville in 1856, Mokelumne Hill in 1854 and Georgetown in 1852.

As towns grew, laws were made which specified that streets had to be wide enough to serve as fire lanes. Volunteer fire fighting companies were formed and equipment imported from the East, but in the end it was found that rock and sheet metal were the best protection against fire.

Stone, brick and adobe were used and heavily constructed roofs were often covered with metal and then a thick layer of sand. Metal

Nevada City

shutters were used to protect inflammable materials inside a store should a major fire start in adjoining buildings.

Having noticed the heavy shutters recently on a gold rush store, we asked the present-day general store operator if the building had ever been used as a bank. We were told that the building had always been a store and had managed to escape past fires due to the heavy metal shutters and stone construction. The building is one of two still standing in a block which was at one time solid with stores.

Throughout the Sierra are ruins of buildings which have survived since the gold rush. Many of them appear ready to topple with the first strong wind, but they have managed to hold themselves together, rock upon rock, for as much as 100 years and more.

In one Sierra county town, the only commercial building still standing is the Wells Fargo office. It is built of stone and while it appears to be giving up the ghost by slow degrees, has still outlived frame commercial establishments on the main street of a town which once had a population of 4,000 people.

A type of lava rock was one of the most popular early building materials, but granite was also used. San Francisco's first fireproof building was made of granite from China, but local granite from Quincy was advertised in San Francisco as early as January 1, 1854.

At the height of the gold rush, brick was a popular building material and while much of it was produced in California, there was still a market for Massachusetts brick brought around the Horn.

The chief interest of the early settlers was gold mining, but as life became more settled and as they learned through experience, they began to build the foundation of a state on brick and stone.

—JANUARY 24, 1963

THE TREE PROSPECTOR

There were rocks to climb over and the going was rough as the young Easterner picked his way carefully along Little Grizzly creek. He had come to the Canyon creek area by way of Downieville and had no more provisions than the few cans he carried in a rough sack over his back.

Harry Moore was a tenderfoot. He was a novice not only to the processes of gold mining, but to the processes of living, as well. It's a wonder he ever made it to California.

Harry had been brought up by his mother and had suffered for it. His father had left the meek woman years before and the son had since then been nurtured like a hothouse blossom. It was a surprise not only to Harry's mother and friends that he had finally made the jump into life, but to Harry as well.

He had always read a lot and knew that adventure and a different life were just beyond the reaches of his mother.

"I'm 18 and a man," he had told himself for three weeks solid before he finally got up courage to steal out of the house one night and leave for "Californy."

Reports of the excitement in the Sierra had kindled some dormant spark deep within the young man. By the time he joined a wagon train west, that spark had burst into a bonfire of enthusiasm.

Now as he slowly made his way up the Little Grizzly between Democrat peak to the south and Cloud Splitter peak to the northeast, he was a little less enthused than when he'd left his Ohio city home.

These deep California canyons weren't at all like the ravines back home. It was at least a thousand feet to the top of Cloud Splitter from the bottom of the creek canyon.

"Hey there, young fellow, stop and set." Harry heard the

voice, but couldn't locate the man who had called to him until he searched through the trees just above the creek bank. He walked over.

"What are you doing over here?" Harry inquired. "I thought you got gold from the creek."

Lem Crane's eyes lit up. He had surely found himself a tenderfoot. He looked about cautiously, asked the boy again to "set" and then confided, "That's what most people think, but it ain't so. The easiest gold is back in these trees.

"You see, young fellow, when the water gets real high in this here small canyon, it drops the big nuggets right in among the bark of these pine trees.

"I've prospected most of the good trees, but if you're interested I could sell you half an acre of pine trees that ain't been touched."

Harry jumped at the chance. He had $25 left of the money he'd earned keeping store for a few days in Sacramento. Lem said the trees were worth more, but since Harry was a newcomer he'd be soft and sell out his half acre tree claim for $25.

The young man climbed 17 trees without finding a trace of the yellow riches. He'd followed Lem's advice and torn at bark until his hands were raw and bleeding.

The last tree did him in and he couldn't climb another, gold or no. Headed for the creek to get a cool drink of water, Harry spotted Lem rolling on the creek gravel and writhing in what appeared to be intense pain.

The older man clutched his stomach with both hands and rolled over and over. As he raced to help his new friend, Harry suddenly realized what had seized the older man. He was stopped short by the sound of tearful laughter which spilled from Lem.

The young man first looked dazed, then hurt and finally mad. Harry's career as a tree prospector ended there and then. He was no longer a tenderfoot.

Harry and Lem are pure fiction. However it is a fact that newcomers were convinced more than once that "tree mining" was profitable during California's golden era.

–April 4, 1963

THE CALIFORNIA SLAVE

Elijah Barker was a slave. He had come to California with his master, James Barker, from Georgia. Even though Elijah could have become a free man due to the fact that California was a free state, he chose to keep faith with himself and his God.

Elijah was living in the Downing Ravine area in 1852 when John Steele met him and half a century later told his story.

The slave had not always gone by the name "Barker" since slaves took the name of their master and Elijah had had other masters. He had changed his name three times before he was given to James Barker's wife as a wedding present.

The master was better suited to a slave society than he was to the aggressive, competitive life in the mining camps. After James Barker ran through the money he had brought West with him, he hired his slave out to work for others.

When the slave had earned enough money for his master to afford the return trip to Georgia, James Barker left the mines for his home. Before he left, his slave was made to promise that he would also return to Georgia when he had earned enough for his own passage.

Elijah dug, hauled, panned and sluiced gold from morning 'til night until he accumulated a sizeable amount of gold. He made several gold strikes and it all could have been his, but he was an honorable man.

The slave's friend, John Steele, learned that Elijah had a wife and two children, but the family had been split when the wife and children were sold to a family named "Grove." Elijah often thought of his family back in the South and feared that they might be sold again and he would never see them.

Steel suggested, "Elijah, you have money. You could buy your wife and children from the Groves and all of you live as free people in California."

He had promised Barker that he would return to Georgia and, having lived some 40 years as a slave, couldn't break his promise. Elijah's

Christian religion had made it possible for him to endure slavery, but also bound him to remain a slave. His religion had given him the ability to accept his fate, but had also imposed its code of ethics. He had given Barker his word and must live up to that pledge.

Steele pleaded, argued and reasoned with Elijah to buy his family and bring them to California. Given time, Steele might have won, but word came from Georgia, calling for the slave to return.

Arrangements had been made for Elijah to travel with other Georgians who were returning from California.

Steele made one last plea when the slave came around to bid farewell, but again Steele failed. Elijah broke down and wept for a long time, finally wiped away his tears and said, "The Lord heard me promise that I'd come back and of course I will."

He refused to break his word and by doing so proved himself a better man than his master who could have granted the slave's freedom at any time.

When Elijah left with the Georgians, his head was bowed and his heart was heavy. He had lived for several years in California as a free man and could fully appreciate the difference between his life as a slave and that of free men.

The slave was spared a return to his former position for on the return trip he died. James Barker was given all of Elijah's earnings as a gold miner and, as Elijah feared, his own wife and children were sold again.

It's hard to understand how one man could buy or sell another, but the practice goes back to the beginning of civilization. We can't help but feel that with centuries of slavery behind us, great progress has been made in the past 100 years.

—July 5, 1963

THE MINERS' DOCTOR

It was but a few weeks before Christmas, 1849, and Silas Jones lay in his tent, near death. He had been unable to work his Middle Creek claim for a week. He lay back on his blankets while the other miners headed for their river diggings each morning.

Silas had gradually been losing the use of his arms and legs until by the end of the week he was limited to one position of rest. He could lie only on his back and look up a scant few feet to the rough, canvas shelter roof.

Help arrived on the eighth day in the form of "Dr. Stephen Cline," a former wheelwright turned miner and most recently doctor.

"Well, let's see what we can do here," the "doctor" said to his patient in a soothing tone, designed to set the miner at ease.

Silas heard "Dr. Cline" prescribe a medicine for him and watched his tent mates as they agreed to give the sick man the proper dosage at the regular, prescribed intervals.

Despite his suffering a small smile played at the corners of Silas's swollen, cracked lips. He smiled again the next day after taking a dose of his medicine and once again, just before he died.

The good doctor brushed off the loss of his patient as due to the fact that he had been called in too late. It could have been the case in the instance of Silas's death, but since the doctor had already lost five other patients in the past month, it appeared more than coincidence.

"Dr. Cline" wasn't the only unlicensed medical practitioner operating in the camps during the early days of the gold rush. Quite a number of men found there was more and easier money to be made doctoring the many miners who became ill in the camps than there was in mining.

These doctors-without-portfolio generally carried a selection of cutlery in one saddlebag and medicines in another. They packed enough hardware to cut anything loose from a hangnail to a left thigh bone.

Small glass bottles and little pill boxes were generally stuffed with harmless enough medicines whose main ingredients were either calomel or castor oil. Patients were told to take a medicine at specified intervals and in regular amounts when it would have made little difference whether they had taken the remedies or not.

It was a disease called "land scurvy" which did poor Silas Jones in and which struck down many another miner of the early camps. The victim's limbs would swell to enormous size and skin color would darken to a deep purple.

Arms and legs became useless due to contraction of muscles and tendons. In many cases gums became enlarged and took on a sickening, gangrenous appearance. The scurvy is thought to have been brought on by lack of vegetables in the diet and abundance of salty, greasy foods.

Rheumatism, sciatica, fever, ague and pulmonary diseases—other common ailments of the first miners—were thought to have resulted from sleeping in damp clothes on the cold ground.

"Dr. Cline" was asked to leave the Middle Creek diggings soon after Silas's death since the "doctor" was unable to produce his diploma from a medical school. He claimed to have left it back East rather than take a chance on losing it in the wilderness. Few of the miners believed the "good doctor" and insisted that he leave while still able.

On his departure, an old mountain man stepped in and served as medical advisor without pay, clearing up many of the milder cases of scurvy through a diet of moderation and common sense.

"Dr. Cline" probably gave up his practice and resorted to plain, hard work after deciding there were fewer perils in mining than in doctoring.

–July 19, 1963

THE FIRST MILLIONAIRE

California's first millionaire, Sam Brannan, made money as if it were his own invention. He is credited with spreading the first news of the 1848 gold strike, of bringing law and order to San Francisco and with building San Francisco from a few mud huts in the sand-hills into the mightiest city on the coast.

Sam Brannan's only problem was that he spent money like it was going to be declared illegal before the dawn of another day. As might be expected, he died penniless.

Brannan left New York City in February, 1846, leading a group of 238 Mormons from the East to California where they hoped to found a new center for their religion. The party left aboard the ship Brooklyn which Brannan chartered not knowing where the money would come from to pay the group's passage.

Aboard was a printing press which had been used in New York by Brannan to print Mormon papers. There was also a large quantity of seed, mill and farm equipment.

Brannan had been charged by Brigham Young to lead the group of eastern Mormons to the West coast while Brigham directed the evacuation of Mormons from Illinois and Missouri.

Brigham Young's overland group crossed the Mississippi on their way west the same day Brannan's ship pulled anchor for California.

Later differences between Brannan and the Mormon leader over the site of their western center led to Sam's break with the church. For a time after his group arrived in San Francisco, following a harrowing six months' sea voyage, Sam continued as head of the Mormon church on the West coast.

Struck by the opportunities in California, he refused to believe the church had a better chance for survival at the Great Salt Lake. Brigham argued that the necessity to fight for survival in a harsh land wanted by no one else would build the church even stronger while the soft life in California would mark the end of the Mormons.

History notes that Brigham Young was right and Sam wrong, for the

Church of Jesus Christ of Latter-day Saints did prosper in the Utah wilderness. In any event, Young refused to budge and Sam Brannon could not agree with his leader.

Sam went on to establish a store in San Francisco and another at Sutter's Fort. He built the first railroad in California which operated from Sacramento to Folsom and printed the state's first American newspaper, the *California Star*, which had its first edition January 9, 1847.

He organized a company to build the first wharf into San Francisco bay, founded the community of Calistoga which was named after his beloved California and Saratoga of the East. He owned many commercial buildings in his city and organized the first San Francisco vigilantes when cowed law enforcement officers proved ineffectual against the city's hoodlums.

Through a partner operating the Sacramento store at Sutter's, Sam learned that settlers were paying for their purchases with gold. Checking further he discovered the truth about Marshall's January, 1848, gold strike.

According to some historians, Sam is said to have walked through the streets of San Francisco shouting that gold had been discovered on the American river. Whether he actually did or not is unknown, but it is a recorded fact that overland issues of the *California Star* carried the word eastward in April and May, 1848.

With the gold rush, Brannan's earnings multiplied and his desire to spend was scarcely able to keep pace with the rapid growth of capital and holdings.

Divorce in 1870 and a 50-50 cash settlement with his wife forced Brannan to sell his property at a great loss. Ten years later all his holdings were gone and Sam was a penniless man of 51, never able to make a comeback.

He tried land sales in Mexico and in southern California, but couldn't make enough to eat regularly. In his final days he was always in the wrong place at the wrong time. Sam Brannan lived on until 1889 and saw his beloved San Francisco grow into the finest city on the Coast.

He was a vital part of the golden age in the golden state and would have felt right at home in today's California which continually opens new promise of fortunes to be made... and lost.

—August 2, 1963

STATEHOOD

The United States Congress has never been too concerned over setting speed records when it has come to tackling delicate issues. In the case of the early Americans in California, Congress moved too slowly and the settlers helped solve their own problems of statehood.

Dr. John Marsh, John Sutter, Thomas Larkin and others of the old-time Californians had fought to save the state from Mexican rule. Sutter, a Swiss, hadn't been as particular about California becoming a part of the United States as he was about the establishment of a strong system of law and order. He probably would have thrown-in with any government to gain protection for his vast land holdings.

Military governors headed the territorial government of California after independence from Mexico was settled, but Congress kept dragging its feet over the question of proposed statehood. Then, as today, racial equality was a major issue.

From 1848 until September, 1850, when California was finally admitted, anti-slave politicians argued against the pro-slavers until they were blue in the face. Then as now, the politicians solved the problem by a compromise which held the number of slave states to 15 and the anti-slave states to the same number.

Peter H. Burnett

This stalemate could have continued another 50 years and California would have remained a territory but for the energetic settlers who threatened to set up their own "independent Pacific Republic unless they were admitted."

Officials were elected throughout the territory in August, 1849, to attend a September 1, 1849, meeting in Monterey. At the September meeting, elected delegates drew up a bill of rights, set boundaries, chose a capital and designed a great seal for their Republic, state or whatever it was to become.

Those hardy souls also determined that they were to be a free state and, "that neither slavery nor involuntary servitude, unless as punishment for crimes, shall ever be tolerated in this state."

The boundaries set forth by that group are the present state boundaries, the great seal has remained the same and slavery has never been legal in California. The men did make one error. San Jose was chosen as their capital city.

John Sutter

The pioneers and newcomers who worked toward admission had a year to wait before Congress finally approved statehood, but with threats of an independent republic there was little the Congress could do but admit California and on its own terms.

Sutter was given the opportunity to become first governor, but he declined to run for the office, arguing that the press of his own affairs was more than he could handle at that time.

Despite his protests, Sutter's name was placed on the ballot and even though he did no campaigning, he still placed third in the November, 1849, election. Peter H. Burnett, Sutter's attorney, was elected first governor.

By the following September 9, 1850, Congress upset the balance of free and slave states by formally admitting rich California as a free state.

Had those early leaders not been men of courage, convictions and action, statehood might well have waited another decade or longer.

–August 22, 1963

PROTECTING THE CLAIM

The day was dusty-hot and the brown hills so parched that Abel Crane could hardly work up enough spittle to clear his dry mouth. He'd slogged over 20 footsore, wearying miles from the newly-named town of Marysville on the Feather River to the Honcut Creek area of Yuba county.

Crane had come this way in search of gold after making enough for a stake from his Yuba river claim. The man's name wasn't really Crane, but since history fails to record what it might be, we'll attach that one to him in order to tell the story of the Honcut Creek mines.

Abel's pace was a slow, measured one as he crossed the low foothills and until he reached a game trail leading into Honcut Creek Canyon.

On reaching the creek he got down on his knees, scooped up a drink of water, then splashed the clear liquid over his face and head. Abel was not addicted to personal cleanliness so he didn't go any farther than to splash just enough water to cool himself.

Bent over at the stream, he watched a lizard dart behind a rock. Abel looked carefully about to make certain there were no rattlers nearby. Satisfying himself that all was safe, he took another drink of water then rose and started upstream.

Knowing that there could be Indians nearby, he worked his way carefully up the stream. After a half hour of following the creek, he noticed that the water was getting muddier. Abel realized that he was not the first miner in the area.

Rounding a bend in the stream, he stopped dead in his tracks and gaped at the sight of Indian gold miners, at least 20 of them, working industriously with pans, rockers and shovels. It was the first time Abel had seen foothill Indians show enough ambition and energy to do more than run off after thieving a white man's blankets or food.

With the Indians, and evidently directing their work, was a white man. Seeing a member of his own race, Abel Crane brightened. If he weren't the first man to prospect this area, he could at least get in on what must be rich diggings, judging from the number of Indians at work.

He walked over to the stranger and introduced himself. "I'm Abel Crane and intend to do some panning in these parts. Looks like you've got things set up the way they was meant to be, with the heathens a-working for you."

The stranger didn't appear too happy to see Crane and barked, "Brown's the name, Major Brown, and these Indians are all my friends, Crane. I help them and they help me."

"Nothing to get touchy about. If you'd just as soon not have company, I'll leave you and your Indians alone and stake my claim upstream," Crane retorted, miffed at not being welcomed by a man who appeared to enjoy the company of Indians to that of his own kind.

Major Brown studied the man carefully, gave him a long, hard look and then, while holding his rifle pointed upstream, said in an icy, level tone, "My claim goes as far up this river as this rifle bullet will carry, Crane, and I expect that's quite a ways."

Abel got the point and backed off with a brief goodbye, resolved to get back to the quiet Yuba where folks weren't so fussy about company.

Major Brown scared off competition from that first prospector, but others followed and by 1851 camps had spring up in the Honcut Creek area. Natchez, named after the Mississippi river town, was one and Hansonville, which had as many as 1,000 residents, was another. Hansonville later became Rackerby and can still be found on state maps. Most of the other communities of this area have long since disappeared.

Major Brown had arrived at Honcut Creek in 1850 and found the stream to be a good producer through the following two years. There was a decline in mining in that area from 1853 until 1858 when there was another brief spurt of activity.

After 1860 the Yuba county region where Major Brown worked with his Indians faded with many another foothill locale where gold was the cornerstone.

—September 12, 1963

A WEALTH OF RICHES

Early settlers came to California across the prairies, through deserts and then over the rough barrier of the Sierra Mountains. They traveled through what we now consider the finest vacation land in the world.

Today we seek the controlled discomfort of outdoor camping and are happy to spend time and money seeking the same desert and mountains the early settlers suffered through.

Imagine a wagon train of Midwestern immigrants fighting through the Nevada desert, reaching the sharp eastern wall of the Sierra and then battling hand over hand, step by step up the mountain side. Wagons were double and triple teamed to pull them up the easy slopes. Blocks and tackle were used in the more difficult climbs and in many cases where the hills was overhung or vertical, wagons were abandoned and the settlers came ahead on foot.

These people were of every type, manner, religion, background and inclination and there must have been a number who appreciated the beauty of the country even though they were "breaking their backs" trying to live through it.

Downieville

In 1849, Dr. David G. Webber, then 41 years old, came West, settling in Downieville where he temporarily gave up his practice of medicine in favor of gold mining.

The doctor had been impressed with the Sierra Nevada Mountains and eventually came to realize that recreation might become of more value to California than gold.

In 1852 Dr. Webber staked a claim at Truckee Lake on the Henness Pass road although there was no evidence of any mineral wealth in that immediate area. He did little to develop his property and in 1854 moved from Downieville to the Sacramento valley.

He stayed in the valley until 1859 when he moved back to the mountains, establishing a medical practice and opening a drugstore at Sierra Valley. The doctor also found time to operate a cattle ranch.

The next year, in 1860 he built a hotel at his Truckee lake property, stocked the lake with trout and put in a small fleet of rowboats.

Henness Pass was an important mountain highway at the time, carrying a great deal of traffic from California shipping points to the Nevada silver mines.

The doctor's hotel was at nearly the 7,000 foot level and in beautiful surroundings. Bridle paths were chopped out of the forest and with his trout, boats and natural wild game, one of our first resort operators was in business.

As is the case with many resort owners who enter the business because of their own love for the outdoors rather than business acumen, the doctor made little money. He couldn't bring himself to charge enough for the services he offered.

The doctor had many guests who came to stay at his hotel or who based their camp at Truckee Lake. It may seem surprising that the overland immigrants who but a few years before had cursed the great outdoors, came to the doctor's mountain retreat in large numbers.

They enjoyed the same "comforts" we do today. There were skinned knees, a few broken bones, many mosquito bites, cold nights on hard ground and few conveniences. Men went for days without shaving and delicate women had a hard time keeping their hair in place and their hands in lily-white condition.

By 1863, Truckee became known as Webber Lake and goes by that name today. There are the same wonders now which made Dr. Webber realize there's more wealth in the Sierra than that which is dug out by pick and shovel and valued by the ounce.

–September 19, 1963

MEADOW LAKE GOLD

When he arrived in the Sierra, Henry Hartley looked more like a soup bone which had barely escaped the dog pack rather than the future founder and last survivor of a teeming mountain city. But then appearances are often deceiving.

Henry suffered from some ailment of civilization and appeared to be near his death bed when he arrived in the northern mining camps in 1860. He made his way to isolated Meadow Lake in Nevada county.

Few men figured that the obviously sick Hartley would last more than a few months and perhaps the isolated lake which lies at the 7,000-foot elevation just 10 miles northwest of Donner Summit was a fitting place for the jump-off into the next world.

Henry reacted as we'd expect most any sick man to act who has been turned loose in the high mountains. He built a cabin, hiked over the hills in fair weather and skiied over them when the winter snow came.

Henry wasn't primarily a gold miner, but hiking over the hills as much as he did it wasn't too much of a surprise that he made a discovery.

In 1863 he came across gold bearing rock just south of his lonesome lake. The sample showed a high percentage of gold and helped him sell two miners on joining with him to form the Excelsior Company.

This modest beginning marked the start of a town which was to have as many as 4,000 residents, 200 businesses—90 of them saloons—and 500 buildings. The town lasted 10 years, had an orderly beginning, a seasonal life and an abrupt, flaming end.

The summer after Hartley's discovery another company moved in and staked nearby claims on what appeared to be an immensely rich ore ledge.

The big boom came when the Comstock went into a temporary decline in 1865. Ten thousand people left Virginia City and it is believed that nearly 3,000 of them moved to Summit City or Meadow Lake.

The camp was known by both names then.

A city was laid out on a 160-acre site and by late summer, 1865, there were 70 houses. By the time winter hit the high-mountain community, 150 houses had been built, but of the thousands of summer residents only some 200 stayed to face the severe winter. The town was incorporated March 24, 1866, and officially named Meadow Lake. There were stamp mills and sawmills nearby, hotels in the town and some brick houses. Four thousand people moved back in the spring. There were 500 buildings in the town that summer. A school had been built and a newspaper operated from Meadow Lake for a short time.

As many as 3,000 people stayed through the winter of 1866-67 and at least 90 per cent of them must have wished they'd headed for the valley below. Snow piled 25 feet in the streets of the town and skiing became one of the major recreations that winter. Snowshoe Thompson made a trip in after one particularly severe storm when no one else could get through to the marooned community.

By spring, 1867, the population bounced back to 4,000 and all this time there had been little or no profit realized from the gold veins and eight stamp mills. While samples assayed high, it was impossible to separate the gold from its host ore. Hope kept the thousands in Meadow Lake and kept others coming back.

A few hundred diehards lingered on into the summer of 1867, among them was Henry Hartley. Less than 100 stayed through the winter of 1868 and there were fewer than 20 people left two years later. Henry was the only one who hung on in 1873, but after all, why should he have left? It was his home.

A fire that September burned most of the houses in the deserted city, but Henry stayed with his memories and a spark of hope that he might yet hit it rich.

He never realized anything from his gold strike nor from the sale of his mine in 1891 for Henry lived only another year before death finally reached out to pluck him from his mountain top.

Some of the other Meadow Lake miners went on to make rich strikes. Henry never did find his fortune, but he at least had 32 years of "wealth" just by being alive in the high Sierra.

—September 26, 1963

EXPRESS DELIVERY

Fable, a little fact and a lot of fiction have combined to give the impression today that the highways and trails of early California were thick with outlaws. This wasn't necessarily the case. One of the state's early expressmen commented that he lost more money through "crooked help" than he ever did to outlaws.

Todd and Company was the express outfit and Todd complained that one clerk made off with $70,000, another with $50,000 and a more considerate one with only $40,000.

When you stop to think about it, Todd may have been something of a highwayman in his own right. When he began his express company, Todd charged an ounce of gold for delivering a letter between the southern mines and San Francisco.

Gold was first worth $14 an ounce and then $16 at San Francisco. It was valued at less than that by $2 to $8 an ounce at the mines, but a rate of from $6 to $14 per letter was just a little steep, no matter how you look at it. Todd could afford to lose a little to several clerks and still stay ahead of the game.

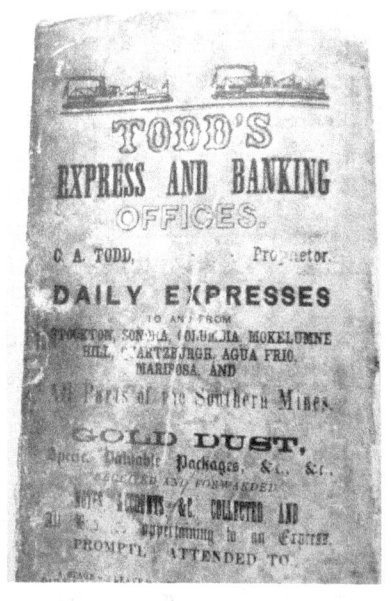

The express business was an efficient one in California and for a time took business away from the postal system which was unable to provide fast enough service for the pioneer miners and settlers.

C. L. Cody, who offered a weekly service from San Francisco to Sutter's Fort as early as July, 1847, is believed to be the first California expressman. Cody's venture was short lived since there was little use for his services at that time.

Expressing started in the Eastern states as late as 1834 with Alvin Adams, Henry Wells and William G. Fargo noted as being pioneers in the business.

Sam Brannan opened the first overland express service after the gold rush when he sent copies of his newspaper, the *California Star*, plus some letters to the East. Sam began his service on April 1, 1848, by sending copies of his paper which told about the gold strike in January of that year at Sutter's sawmill.

Brannan's express didn't last long, but others came along, including Todd and Company. Todd soon found that carrying gold dust was his most profitable venture. He charged five per cent commission for carrying the valuable merchandise.

Todd's headquarters were in Stockton and his company managed to survive thieving clerks, lasting until 1851 when it was sold, to eventually become a part of the successful Adams and Company express service.

Adams and Company was operated as a California concern, but was closely connected with the strong eastern company by the same name. Adams in California failed in the business panic of 1855.

Todd had a part ownership in another successful express company known as Reynolds, Todd and Company. This line eventually became a part of another concern, Wells Fargo and Company. As any Californian knows, Wells Fargo weathered not only the panic of 1855, but every other financial crisis since then and lives today in the California banking company.

One of the earliest expressman tells of grossing about $1,000 a day hauling gold dust on two horses. He had little trouble with outlaws and at his earning rate could probably have easily stood a loss or two.

California expressmen operated under some of the most difficult conditions to be found in the country. They showed their ingenuity by using every conveyance from burros, horses, mules, dog sleds or two strong legs to insure the commercial growth of the state.

–October 3, 1963

THE DOG EXPRESS

The express run from Quincy to LaPorte was challenging, invigorating and inspiring although rough going in places during summer months of the 1850's. In the winter it was a next-to-impossible route.

Before year-round auto and rail transportation came to Plumas County, expressmen managed to operate on schedule through summer or winter to supply the needs of miners and townspeople in the Feather River country.

From Quincy to Nelson's Point, travel was a breeze. From there on to the top of the ridge was a slow climb for horses pulling heavy wagons or Concord coaches. Summer travel along the Gibsonville ridge was picturesque, awe inspiring and dangerous at times, but it was possible.

From Little Grass Valley on into LaPorte the route was an easy one, but during the winter months the whole trip was next to impossible.

Despite the fact that roads weren't kept open and the snow seems to lie deeper in this area than most any other in Northern California, Whiting and Company managed to make regular express deliveries from Quincy to LaPorte and back, summer or winter, on schedule.

The Quincy-based firm relied on horses and mules in the summer, but when these sturdy animals floundered belly-deep in wet, clinging, heavy snow, Whiting switched to dog sleds.

Whiting started his business in 1857 with a partner, H. C. Everts, of Everts and Company, a LaPorte to Marysville line. With Everts in the LaPorte-Marysville concern was another family member, F. D. Everts, who had started his business in 1851.

Chico was supply base for Whiting and Company, Marysville for Everts and Company.

It is doubtful if any other express company of the 1850's relied on dogs to haul supplies, gold dust and mail during the winter months.

Whiting started with heavy mongrels and gradually added New-

Horse Snowshoes

foundlands and St. Bernards to his "stable" until he had sturdy animals who could work in heavy snow, hitched two or four to a team.

One writer claims that Whiting used four dogs to pull 250 pounds of express and one person. Another states the dogs hauled loads which were often over 600 pounds.

There is also some disagreement over the length of time the dogs remained in service, but they did operate in the winter of the mid 1850's over the LaPorte-Quincy route. The present road is not kept open during winters due to heavy snowfalls.

Whiting's Dog Express was in business during the 1850's and possibly as late as 1865. Modern methods came along to finally provide Whiting with a better way of getting things done. The horse snowshoe made it possible for horses and mules to pull passengers and express through the heavy snow and marked the end of the dog express.

One day several years ago, while gazing at the decorations in Riley's LaPorte bar, we saw a horse snowshoe fastened to the wall. We had read descriptions of the device and could see that it must have worked well.

Holes were cut in a metal plate to catch the horseshoe projections and a metal strap fastened with a turnbuckle across each horse hoof to hold the contraption in place. The plate measures approximately 12 inches across by about 14 inches long.

It's doubtful if many horses really enjoyed the devices although we'll have to admit that they must have been "attached" to them. In any event, ingenuity kept mail, supplies and gold dust rolling.

–OCTOBER 10, 1963

COMSTOCK'S GOLD

They called him "Old Pancake." He was a bum who would have sold-out his best friend if the price were right. Because he was one of the noisier misfits in the Nevada camp, the fabulous silver strike which produced more California millionaires than was ever possible with gold became known as the "Comstock."

Henry Thomas Paige Comstock was a Canadian herder who came to the Nevada Gold Canyon area with a flock of sheep around the first part of 1851.

Gold Canyon, at that time, was populated mainly by outcasts fleeing the law, or men who couldn't get along with civilization.

One of the wanted men was "Old Virginny." His name was really James Fennimore, but when he left California one jump ahead of the law, he changed it to "Finney" and then allowed Finney to be corrupted to "Virginny" and finally "Old Virginny."

Comstock was along the night Old Virginny and some of their cronies were wandering through the sagebrush looking for a spot to bed down. The boys had hoisted a few too many at the bar and were unsteady.

Old Virginny, the unfortunate, dropped his bottle of red eye, searched through the undergrowth and found that it had broken. With a rare presence of mind reserved solely for scholars and drunks, he held up a broken remnant of the bottle and announced, "I christen you Virginia Town."

His drink partners thought it was a great idea and decided they would have a settlement at Virginia Town. From that humble beginning sprang the mightiest of all the mining camps and the modern tourist mecca, Virginia City.

There had been sporadic mining in the Gold Canyon area of Nevada (then Utah territory) since the first of the California-bound '49ers stopped to pan a nugget or two. Some of the nuggets were of a fair size, but most of the pioneers couldn't wait to push on to California where "gold was to be found at every bend in every stream."

The misfits began assembling in the spring of 1851. They had overstayed their welcomes in California and felt safe in desolate Gold Canyon. Living wasn't too hard. With a minimum of work a man could literally dig up the price of a bottle and manage to forget that scenery wasn't everything.

The biggest mining problem in Gold Canyon was the "blue stuff" in which the gold occurred. It was a strange ore with a blue cast. Mexican miners early guessed the ore was silver, but no one listened to them. Allen and Hosea Grosch, in 1851, realized that the ore was silver, but they could never get enough of a stake to exploit their claims.

Comstock suspected that the Grosch boys had stumbled on to something, but failed to learn what it was. Even after he went through the Grosch's personal papers on their death, he was unable to fathom the secret.

Henry Comstock

The riches of the Comstock went unknown until 1859 when an assay finally revealed the true nature of the blue ore.

Comstock was still on the trail of gold and not silver when he traded a blind horse to Old Virginny for the latter's interest in what was to become a multimillion dollar property, the Ophir mine.

Old Pancake later sold out his interest for $11,000 and couldn't stop bragging how he'd tricked the "slick Californians" by unloading his claim at a tremendous profit.

The first load of ore hauled by pack mules to San Francisco brought more than enough profit to pay for Comstock's share of the Ophir.

For a man who was a bum any way you looked at him, Comstock did achieve a measure of fame. His name has come down through the past 100 years of history to designate the greatest strike of them all.

–OCTOBER 17, 1963

THE ST. LOUIS SCHOOLHOUSE

Jamie McGrath dawdled through his breakfast and wished that he could do anything but go to school that crisp, clear morning. There were deer moving through the hills and miners would be washing gold from gravel near town.

St. Louis was a bustling Sierra county community by 1857 and Jamie was a bustling 9 year-old who had more important things to do than go to school.

He lived just outside St. Louis on the road to Howland Flat. His father had built their two-room, frame house soon after the family arrived at the camp from their Missouri farm.

Everything here was new to Jamie. There were trees which didn't grow in his native state. Deer were plentiful and he saw an occasional bear nearby. The birds were even different than the ones he had known in Missouri. There hadn't been anything like a gold mining camp "back home" and to Jamie each day was a new experience. There were men digging in deep pits, hauling out gravel and washing it to recover small flakes of metal.

The long mule trains which wound past his house on their way from LaPorte (Rabbit Creek then) to Howland Flat, Potosi, Poker Flat and the other camps farther back in the hills were a fascinating sight.

All of it was new except school. That seemed to be the same in California as in Missouri. St. Louis, which was founded by a group of Missourians in the fall of 1852 on the site of Sears' Diggings, an earlier camp, had not neglected education.

By 1853 a 20-pupil school was in operation and it was to this school that Jamie set off after breakfast.

"I wish the old schoolhouse would burn down," he muttered as he kicked a loose rock ahead of him down the well-worn wagon trial. Similar sentiments have been expressed ever since there were schoolboys and despite all the power they have been able to conjure through wishful thinking, very few schools have burned down as a result.

California pioneers felt deeply about education and set out at an early date to bring culture to the frontier. It has been estimated that there were no more than 6,000 school age children in the entire state in 1852. Most of the early schools were private ones, but Nevada County had as many as four public schools for its 250 school age children in 1851. Two of the schools were in Grass Valley and two in Nevada City.

By 1859 there were 15 schools in Nevada County for some 600 pupils. Plumas County created three school districts as early as 1854 and there was at least one well-attended school in Downieville by 1856.

If Jamie had known of all the efforts being made to educate him and the other children of the camps, he still wouldn't have been impressed. This day he would just as soon the schoolhouse burned to the ground.

As he lazied along past manzanita and buck-brush the idea became so consuming that he thought he actually smelled smoke. He raced ahead to a clearing where he could see the town. It was smoke. His fondest dream was realized.

It wasn't only the schoolhouse burning; the whole town was ablaze. While he watched through the rest of the morning, most of the town burned to a crisp. The camp later made a brief recovery during the heyday of hydraulic mining in the 1860's, but for all practical purposes, the fire of 1857 killed St. Louis. And what of Jamie? He went ahead to finish school in the next town where the family moved. But he'd at least had his moment of glory.

—October 25, 1963

MISSOURI TREKKERS

Missouri had been a frontier boundary for many years and was not only a jumping-off place for the first Western bound travelers, but also supplied the know-how to mine California's gold.

Trappers bound for the upper Missouri River basin operated from St. Louis during the early 1800's. Ashley and Henry led beaver trappers as far west as the Great Salt Lake and north into the Snake River County from their St. Louis headquarters.

Another trapper who added a great deal of new information to the store of western geographic knowledge was Jedediah Smith. Jedediah and two partners succeeded Ashley and Henry in the fur trade, still maintaining a home base at St. Louis.

Smith, in 1826, became the first American to travel overland to California and later mapped the length of the state after trekking north into Oregon.

Dr. John Marsh, first American doctor to arrive in California (1836), stayed to make it his home. Marsh, a New Englander by birth, was highly educated, but preferred living on the edge of civilization. He had come from the upper reaches of the Northwest Territory, been in Illinois a short while and moved on to Missouri where he operated a retail store.

He came to California from Independence, Missouri, by way of Santa Fe, New Mexico.

Determined to see his adopted land become a part of the United States, Marsh encouraged settlers to join him in the golden land. He began, in 1840, a letter writing campaign urging his Missouri friends to join him in the land of eternal springtime.

His letters were quoted and reprinted in Missouri newspapers. Some letters appeared in print as far east as New York state.

Marsh drew on information gathered by Jedediah Smith and other pathfinders to provide rough maps for his Missouri friends to follow on the overland journey.

Missourians were enthused and hundreds signed to make up the first wagon train of immigrants. Of the large number of enthusiasts only 69 set out in the spring of 1841 for Marsh's promised land.

John Bidwell, one of the 69, later reported that California looked like anything but a land of "eternal spring" when his party arrived in November, 1841. The Missouri group reached Marsh's ranch which was

located at the base of Mt. Diablo during a time of drought. Not a drop of water had fallen during the previous 18 months and the land obviously looked more like the shades of hell than anything else.

(If this weather report is correct it means that the central valley had missed an entire rainfall season.)

Being on the edge of the wilderness when word was received that gold had been discovered in the Sierra, Missourians were among the first to reach California in that deluge of 1849.

Lead mining in Missouri dated back to as early at 1798. A smelter at Potosi, Missouri, made the lead shot used in the War of 1812. The lead miners brought not only know-how to the Sierra gold fields, but even their own St. Louis and Potosi.

St. Louis in Sierra County was founded on the Gibsonville Ridge by a group of Missourians. Potosi was but a few miles away, near Howland Flat. The sites of Potosi and St. Louis are still marked, but little other proof of their existence remains.

The more lasting influence of the Missourians is their heritage of strength handed down by men who left their own state for the unknown.

–NOVEMBER 14, 1963

ONION VALLEY WINTER

The howling wind struck Onion Valley, roared through the collection of board and canvas shacks like an express train, shuddered to a hesitating stop and then blasted back from the opposite direction. Only the day before it had been summer in the Sierra.

Bone-rattling winter came to Onion Valley and none of the miners, storekeepers or other miscellaneous characters who made up the roster there were prepared for it.

Gold discovery didn't leave much time for the niceties of life. There were too many seeking the precious metal and the atmosphere throughout the mountains was one of rush, hurry and grab before all the gold was gone.

Few men took the time to build permanent houses. That would have to come later. For the time they settled for canvas and cloth brush shelters. A few men insisted on a real house and put together plank or log cabins, but even they were easily satisfied. A few cracks in the wall or light visible through the roof meant little to them.

The chilling blast which flashed through the canyon and back again savored Onion Valley much as a gourmet sips his wine, mouths a tender morsel of prime ribs or lingers over a strong, thick cup of aromatic coffee.

The sky remained black through the morning and only the hardiest miner ventured out to work his rocker or pan. By early afternoon the wind died to a mild howl and the sun broke through for minutes at a time. Soft, white snowfall began that night.

By the next morning there was a four-inch covering over brush huts, cabins, and the hillsides about the flat. What had been a miserable summer picture became a scene of exaggerated beauty. Flapping tatters draped over trimmed manzanita lend little charm to the landscape, but add wind-sculptured snow and the scene changes to one reminiscent of picture postcard perfection.

Harsh lines of plank hovels and cabins were softened and a water bucket left outside a cabin assumed an air of grace with its stately hat of white.

The cloth shelters which dotted the flat and hillsides became igloos which appeared to have been built by inebriated Eskimos. The charm of the north country came to Onion Valley that winter of 1850, but those first miners, unlike the Eskimos, new little about becoming part of the cold. They suffered with a passion.

Few thought of mining gold the day after the snow fell. Partners huddled together, blankets draped over them in whatever shelter they had, cursing the miserable weather that kept them from their diggings.

Through the day the wind blew with a fury, driving icy flecks of snow from the top of the ridge into the flat where it swirled down and then up again. The wind stopped only long enough to drop more snow, then rearranged the landscape hourly as though to fit the mood of a playful, giant sculptor.

Mining came to a halt and most of the miners decided that a foothill claim would be preferable to battling the savage forces in the higher mountains.

Weeks later Mother Nature showed her fickle, feminine side by relaxing long enough for men to come back that winter and chop out more gold from the frozen gravel. On January 1, 1851, over $6,000 was taken from one deposit in just an hour and a half. Other rich finds were made and before the year was over 1500 men had settled at Onion Valley.

The harsh wind still pours off the rim and into the valley as it did 100 years ago when it reminded the men of 1850 that they could be sent packing in a minute as so many unwelcome guests.

–NOVEMBER 21, 1963

THE HYDRAULIC FLOODS

Frank Parks operated a store in Marysville during the flood of 1875 and he bitterly wished the Sierra gold miners had never been so cussed inventive.

Frank Parks wasn't really the storekeeper's name, but we'll call him that for want of a better one. That January day in 1875 Frank was busy hauling everything off his floor and onto counter tops, shelves or any place else where it would be safe from water which was coming through the front door of his store.

Marysville's 1849 settlers believed they had picked the most likely spot for their town when they located along the banks of the Yuba River near its confluence with the Feather. The Yuba was said to be 70 feet deep where it passed the town and that seemed enough of a channel to hold any stream.

It could have been except for the imagination of the Sierra miners who conjured up water snorting demons which washed sand, gravel, gold and trees from the hillsides and into downstream channels.

A previous flood, in 1853, had plagued Marysville storekeepers by splashing water into many of their stores and damaging a few thousand dollars of merchandise, but the addition of 12 feet of ground fill was expected to take care of any future floods. The expensive filling and grading could have done the trick if it hadn't been for the hydraulic miners of the 1860's and 70's.

Seeking to wash ancient river beds from the mountains they had settled on the water cannon as the ideal answer. Water had been used for years in gold pans, rockers and sluice boxes to separate the heavier gold from gravel, but nothing as ambitious as wholesale removal of a mountain top had been possible until the appearances of the high pressure cannons.

Water from the highest elevations in the gold mining regions was held behind a reservoir and then shot downhill through both open flumes and boiler plate pipe into the cannon where pressure was further increased by reducing the nozzle opening.

A counterbalance loaded with heavy rocks helped to aim the gun against a hillside and off downstream boiled mud, murk and every sort of rubble. The gold was taken out in large sluices and the debris sent on its way to fill valley river channels.

By January, 1875, the 70-foot deep channel had been filled with debris necessitating construction of levees around Marysville to protect it from the often-violent Yuba. In places the town was lower than the new river bed and had only the thin levees for protection.

The levees did fail that January, 1875, and Marysville was flooded with water reaching four and five-foot depths in some parts of the town.

The impact of the flood helped bring about legislation to stop hydraulic mining, but the outcries from Marysville were only one small protest among all the others which were being heard in legislative chambers. The protests gradually built into a full scale clamor against the destruction brought on by the cannons.

The federal anti-debris act of 1883 was the resulting legislation which stopped the damage and a court case the following year proved the law was going to stick, but it was too late for Frank Parks and the other flooded Marysville merchants of 1875.

–December 5, 1963

WHEN LOLA CAME TO GRASS VALLEY

City girls sometimes make good campers, but most of them should be left back among the glittering lights and comforts of civilization. This is a simple fact of life that holds as true today as it did over 100 years ago.

Alonzo Delano, a successful Grass Valley businessman and writer, learned that city girls and the outdoors don't mix when he took the famous Spanish dancer, Lola Montez, camping in 1854.

Lola, who was 36 then, had quite a reputation by the time she moved to Grass

Lola Montez

Valley. When she moved to the mountains in 1854 she had already been married three times and had been the companion of King Louis I of Bavaria at age 28.

The beautiful Lola was born Maria Dolores Eliza Rosanna Gilbert and had performed in England and Europe after leaving her native Ireland.

King Louis, an old man with young ideas, had made her the Comtese de Landsfeld shortly after she became his companion in 1846. Palace intrigue got the best of the fiery Lola and she was forced to flee Bavaria for England until she came to America. By 1853 she was playing to packed crowds in San Francisco.

Some reviewers claimed she was a "poor dancer and worse actress" and there must have been some truth to the charge for she decided early the next year to retire from the stage. It was then she moved to Grass Valley where she set local society matrons astir and their husbands possibly even more astir.

It was here that she met Alonzo, then a bachelor and gay man-about-town. Alonzo Delano used the pen name "Old Block" for his collection of stories, "Chips Off the Old Block" and "Life on the Plains and Among the Diggings." Old Block became known as Lola's "secretary" and was one of the most prominent admirers to gather about the beautiful and notorious dancer.

Alonzo was a New Yorker, who had come overland to California in 1849 and first prospected along the Yuba and Feather Rivers and then operated a produce business in San Francisco. Neither venture was particularly marked with success. He later became superintendent of a Grass Valley mine and then was manager of the Adams Express company bank in Grass Valley until he opened his own bank there in 1855.

A Grass Valley newspaper in July, 1854, announced that Lola, Old Block and a mixed party of men and women were off to the mountains for a stay of three weeks. It probably seemed like a great idea to the entire group while planning the trip from a comfortable Grass Valley living room, but once in the hills it was a different story.

Camped on Truckee Pass, Lola's hot Spanish-Irish blood froze solid and the weather, coupled with other discomforts of camp, aroused her to upbraid Alonzo fiercely. She not only scared him off, but the mule skinner and camp tender as well who stole away with all the food and pack animals. Lola's and the rest's three-week campout was condensed to one.

As a result of the trip, two lakes, Upper and Lower Lola, were named for the dancer and years later another lake, Independence, was re-named for her. A mountain peak which Alonzo had named "Moore's Peak," was changed to Mt. Lola.

Alonzo learned his lesson about city girls and soon after married and in later years took his wife and young daughter to Webber Lake for more proper family outings.

Lola left Grass Valley in 1855, but her mark still remains on the country which she disliked so vehemently.

–December 12, 1963

SIERRA CHRISTMAS

(This week's column departs from the usual factual history of early California to bring a fictional story of Christmas in one Sierra mining camp of the 1850's.)

It was still two days before Christmas at Cutthroat Bar and for Yancey Crane it might as well have been Chinese New Year. The one holiday meant as much to him as the other.

Yance was a loner who was civil to no man and had no family to recall in fond reminiscences. When he was roaring drunk which wasn't too frequent by Cutthroat Bar standards, he thought of his Missouri childhood only to curse the many relatives who had raised him.

He had been orphaned at an early age and had no Christmases to remember. The days he remembered most were ones of abuse, of being handed from one relative to another and never having a home of his own.

At 19 Yance had exerted his last effort to fight back by stealing off to join a California-bound wagon train. Having drawn into himself for so many years he found that he couldn't match wits with the other immigrants and still stood on the outside looking in.

Arriving in Sacramento he'd worked to earn enough for miner's provisions only to find that the shoddy clothes and tools wouldn't stand up under a full day's use at the mines.

Fortunes had been made in the Sierra but Yance had only scraped by and six years after arriving in California he was gradually losing the will to keep trying. Outside the store where he'd cashed in his scant poke of gold dust for a sack of flour, a few scraps of pork and a small bag of beans, he shivered and drew his collar tight against his neck, then trudged off through the cold snow toward his rough cabin with the supplies.

Christmas would be no time of rejoicing for Yancey Crane. "If this snow keeps falling," he thought, "I won't be able to work my claim and may have to call it quits, only Lord knows how I'll ever get through this winter in these forsaken, cold mountains."

Passing the Coleman cabin, Yance stopped and couldn't help but look through the unshaded window. If it could be said Yance had any friend, it was young Tom Coleman who was the only person he'd said more than two words to since he'd been in the camp.

The recently-widowed Sarah Coleman and her dark-haired son were side by side at their table and Yance saw that they had only bread to eat, but both were smiling. He couldn't understand their pleasure until he noticed the young boy point to a scrawny pine tree in a corner of the room.

"They must be talking of Christmas," he grumbled. "The fools—they ought to know better. There'll be no Christmas for them or for me. There's not a soul to look out for them with her old man lying under this frozen soil."

Yance started to walk on, but stopped again and looked to the bright, clear wintery heavens where a single star stood out from all the rest. "Well, I guess it's the least I can do," he muttered to himself and stole back to the Coleman's door where he laid his package of just-purchased food.

After a restless, chilly night and with hunger gnawing inside him, Yance woke and looked about his bare cabin. He was ready to quit. Life had dealt him a hand from an uncut deck and he didn't want to play it out any further. "A 'pair' is a poor poker hand and I wouldn't even have a pair if I had one wild card." It was the bitter end of his rope.

An eager knock roused him and he opened the door to Tom Coleman's bright young face. "Mr. Crane, we're going to have a Christmas party tonight and we want you to come have supper with us. I told Ma that you were my best friend and were all alone and she said I could ask you. Will you come?"

His words blurted out and stunned Yancey Crane, but Yance's despair lifted and he accepted. His star was gone from the daylight sky, but Yance knew he could keep going. Someone had to look out for the widow and her young son and he was the one who could do it.

"They're going to be alright. I know it. Besides three of a kind beats a pair any day." —December 19, 1963

FROM GROWLERSBURG TO GEORGETOWN

San Francisco harbor in 1849 was gradually becoming a graveyard of sailing vessels. Masts swung from side to side and deserted ships bobbed despondently on the changing tide.

There was hardly a seaman to be found in the village by the bay despite the large number of new daily arrivals. Once a ship touched shore, crews deserted in wholesale lots and made their way to the mines. Fortunes were to be made in golden California and neither force nor threats were strong enough to keep the sailors on board ship.

One group which made for the mountains was led by George Phipps for whom the town of Georgetown was named. Phipps and his sailors passed through Sacramento and Auburn and then climbed the 20 miles east to Oregon Creek and Hudson Gulch where a party of Oregonians had begun mining early in 1949.

The first signs of a town near here appeared in 1850 when a group of tents and shacks known as Growlersburg was built downhill from the present Georgetown.

The camp was destroyed by fire, rebuilt and then abandoned in 1852. It was when the miners moved uphill that they dropped "Growlersburg" in favor of "Georgetown," honoring George Phipps and his sailors.

Georgetown prospered and by 1855, when it was known as "the pride of the mountains," had a school, church, theatre, townhall, Sons of Temperance hall, Masonic hall, three hotels and many stores.

Following an 1856 fire which wiped out all the town except for the Masonic hall, Georgetown businessmen determined to prevent future fire losses. An entire block of business buildings was then constructed of brick.

Scotch Broom

By the early 1860's one of the first nurseries in the mining camps was established by a Scotsman at Georgetown. Scotch Broom, which today grows wild in the hills about the town, is said to have sprung from the original nursery plantings. There are also many other plants, unusual for the Sierra, which may be found in local gardens, undoubtedly progeny of the Scotsman's nursery stock.

After the easy gold was taken out of the Placer claims, deep mines continued producing even more wealth. In this area were a number of seam mines where gold was found in quartz and the quartz was interspread through layers of slate.

One of these seam mines, the French claim at Greenwood Valley, yielded $4 million in the 13 years from 1872 to 1885.

Mining was briefly revived here during the 1930 depression years, but no large commercial operation survives. Today the community serves a small population of orchardists, sportsmen, lumbermen and a few independent miners.

Sportsmen help keep Georgetown alive as much as any group for the town is a gateway to excellent hunting, fishing and hiking in the wild Rubicon River and Rubicon Basin country.

–December 26, 1963

LOST IN THE SNOW

Swen Larson stumbled and mumbled in his purple alcoholic fog, pulling one snowshoe after the other through the deep snow.

It had been a clear, cold day that dark morning some 14 hours earlier when Swen left Deer Park Springs for Tahoe City on his way to pick up mail for the snowbound Deer Park resort where he was employed as caretaker.

The ingoing trip would have been a hard hike for anyone not used to Sierra snow-shoeing, but to the rugged Scandinavian it was no more than a brief morning walk.

He had reached Tahoe City in good time, but his unquenchable thirst pulled him into the nearest bar where he drank quite well, but not wisely. It had been some time since he'd been to the settlement and his thirst was a long, deep one which was as much a thirst for townpeople as for the strong, raw brew he gulped down.

He stopped drinking long enough to pick up the mail sack, then bought a jug to take back to Deer Creek, spilled down several more "long ones" and then unsteadily strapped on his snowshoes for the return trip.

Swen hadn't meant to linger in Tahoe City the entire afternoon, but had lost all track of time, distance and space.

With his snowshoes pointed in the general direction of home he set out through the dimly lighted town toward the forest. His head spun and his feet refused to keep any regular pace or rhythm. Swen brushed into a snow covered pine branch and received a wet face full of snow which he neither felt nor saw. He sat down a few long minutes, took a pull from his jug, then another and managed to get to his feet again.

As his body warmed from the exertion of stumbling and sliding over the hard crust, Swen loosened his coat and tossed his hat to the ground. He vaguely noticed that it was the warmest night he'd remembered in a long time.

Behind him silently appeared a gaunt wolf that sensed the man was some sort of "wounded animal" with but a little longer to go. Another wolf, then another joined the first and soon a pack of six animals trailed the reeking Swede.

Moon broke through the clouded sky and made a light for the stage on which was played the primitive drama of man against wilderness. On slogged Swen until he finally gave up completely after tripping into a deep snow bank. His mind cleared for several minutes and he remembered who he was and why he was there, but the combination of alcohol and deep, penetrating cold which had slowed his body was more than he could conquer.

He gave up quietly and completely to the soft, warm, comforting snowbank which nestled him closer than his straw ticking ever had.

The wolves stood back as long as they could and then nosed closer, drooling and snapping in anticipation of the marinated feast which would be theirs.

It was several days before a rescue party set out to look for the wayward mail carrier and they had little trouble locating him. Swen had wandered some from his usual trail, but the searchers found his mutilated body in the snow along Bear Creek. The remains were kept in cold storage until the following spring when Swen was buried beside the road leading into Deer Park Springs.

(Swen's name is fictitious, but the event took place in the locale mentioned during the winter of 1909).

–JANUARY 3, 1964

THE DUBIOUS HONOR

William S. Bodey worked hard for 11 long years in California mining camps before making his big strike, but lived only a few months to enjoy his new wealth.

Bodey was the prospector for whom the town, "Bodie," was named. Spelling of the town name was changed, but Bodey had little cause for complaint for the town grew up after his death.

The unlucky miner's history as told by a partner is misleading. The man said that Bodey came around the Horn in 1848 and left a 17-year-old son and 19-year-old daughter back in New York state with his wife. When Bodey discovered gold in July, 1859, in the spot called Taylor's Gulch, he was supposed to have been about 45 years old. Figuring backwards he must have been around 15 when his daughter was born. Either that or his friend was a poor judge of age. In any event, facts of his age detract little from Bodey's story.

Bodey and three partners had crossed Sonora Pass to the eastern side of the Sierra and it was there he struck it rich at a spot just northwest of the present ghost town of Bodie.

Bodey and one of the partners, Black Taylor, stayed at the site in a

Bodie State Historic Park

rough cabin they had built, planning to spend the winter in the mountains.

Running low on supplies in November they left for Monoville and were caught in a blizzard on their return trip. They abandoned the packs with their food supplies and struggled on blindly, searching for their cabin.

When Bodey's strength failed, Taylor helped him up and carried the man for awhile. Pausing to rest, he was unable to lift Bodey to his shoulders again. Taylor made his friend as comfortable as possible, told him he would be back to get him and set out alone for their cabin.

Taylor was lucky enough to locate the cabin and after resting did go back into the storm for his companion. Hunting all night he still failed to find Bodey. The storm continued for two more days, filling in and smoothing over the spot where Bodey quietly died.

The unhappy Taylor didn't locate his partner's body until spring and from all appearances coyotes had found Bodey first. There wasn't enough of the body left to recognize, but from a knife and other equipment, Taylor identified the remains.

He buried his friend on the spot and soon afterward left for the town of Benton where he settled into another cabin and took up his lonely prospecting. Pauite Indians are said to have killed Taylor during a night raid.

A miner stumbled across Bodey's grave in 1871 when the town was beginning to grow and by 1879—Bodie's boom year when there was a population of 10,000—it was decided that a more suitable burial place for the town's founder was needed.

His meager remains were moved to the town cemetery that fall and it was agreed that a marker should be raised in Bodey's honor.

A sculptor, in 1880, started work on a marker of native granite, but Bodey's name was never chiseled on the stone. When word of President Garfield's death was received in Bodie, townspeople agreed that the marker should be used to honor Garfield's memory and not Bodey's.

The town founder received the dubious honor of burial in the community he made possible, but the site of his grave remains as anonymous as those of the many "slow guns" who rest beside him.

–January 9, 1964

THE STRAWBERRY CONNECTION

More than one mule driver was fooled by Ira Berry, "the tightest man with a dollar on the Washoe trail." They were usually fooled for but a short time and soon learned to keep a close eye on the Strawberry station owner.

"Just look at the barley hanging from the lead mule's mouth. Ol' Berry must have leaded 'em up with a bellyful," the grinning mule whacker commented. When the animal's strength gave out on the hard pull over the Sierra and the same barley was still clinging in suspicious-looking clusters, the mule driver knew he'd been tricked.

Carefully examining the mule's mouth he found that the grain was firmly glued on, and Ira Fuller Berry had undoubtedly seen that something besides grain had gone into the mule's stomach.

Berry eventually got a reputation as a man who seldom gave a mule driver his money's worth. He is said to have fed straw and chaff instead of grain and then put a dab of glue here and there on the animals' mouths. A few kernels of the precious grain were then planted in the glue.

Hay and barley were both valuable commodities on the freighting trail and many outfits set up their own stations with stock feed. Other drivers carried grain in their wagons to beat the high prices.

Both hay and barley sold by the pound, not the ton, on the Washoe trail in the busy summer of 1862. Prices held at five and six cents a pound. Despite the prices there was usually a short supply along the route.

The Strawberry Valley station keeper wasn't content to make what would have been a reasonable profit, but kept up the practice of fooling the mule drivers whenever he was sure of getting away with it. But it wasn't only mule drivers he short changed. Even Berry's guests at the station had to settle for hay or straw instead of feathers in their pillows.

His reputation became bad enough that many drivers would deride

Wild Strawberries

him by calling out, "How about some more straw, Berry!" The expression was so popular that it became a natural assumption of many latecomers that Strawberry Valley and the station were named after the "thrifty" Berry.

It makes a good story and a more colorful one than the actual fact. According to early newspaper records the valley got its name from the abundance of wild strawberries growing in that area. Strawberry Valley was named as early as 1853, some five years before Berry settled in the region.

There's at least one other Strawberry in northern California—this one on the county road which was formerly a wagon trail stretching from Marysville to LaPorte and on to Quincy. There may be more and they probably all owe their names to wild strawberry plants rather than crafty station keepers.

—JANUARY 16, 1964

THE HASTY OPINION

California was much farther from Washington, D.C. and the East in 1865 than it is today, but news of Lincoln's death brought sorrow here as it did there.

At Ford's Theatre in the capital there was pandemonium after the shooting. Later Booth was burned out of a barn where he was discovered days after the shooting. At an isolated way station in the Sierra along Johnson's road to Nevada there was no delay. The station was burned to the ground the night of the assassination and as a direct result of Lincoln's death.

It happened on April 14, 1865, when a small group was spending a quiet evening at Audrain's Station near Lake Tahoe. Over the telegraph line came a message, telling of the president's death.

The general reaction was of sorrow and disbelief although these men had less chance to "know" Abe than we had to know our own assassinated president, John Kennedy. Communications were slower then and Lincoln was exposed to the public in print much less than Kennedy was in our day.

Nonetheless, Lincoln was generally a popular president in the North as well as with some of the more humanitarian southerners.

Thomas Audrain who owned the Sierra station which carried his name, happened to be in sympathy with the South and as he read the message again, burst out with words to the effect, "I'm glad they killed him. It should have happened long ago."

His remarks were taken with about the same stunned silence as would be news

John Wilkes Booth

today that Khrushchev had defected to the Catholic church.

As a man the group arose and faced the jubilant station owner. "We'll give you the chance personally to tell Mr. Lincoln how you feel, Audrain. Fetch a rope, boys, and we'll string him up to the nearest tree."

Audrain fought back desperately, but was easily overpowered. A rope was hauled from the back room and for a minute it appeared that the quick-tongued station keeper was headed for wherever his good and bad deeds had prepared him.

"Hold off a minute," called out a calmer voice. "Hangin's too good for this skunk. Once we hoist him up it'll be all over."

Abraham Lincoln

There was a huddle and then clearer heads prevailed. All the men took everything they owned from the buildings and then, while Audrain was kept tied, set fire to his station.

"He's more apt to remember this," they agreed, "than he'd ever remember a hanging."

After the place was burned to the ground, the station keeper was warned, "If you ever try to build again, we'll come back and finish hanging you to that tree. You can count on that just as sure as you can figure that there'll always be stagecoaches rolling over these mountains."

As you may have noticed, there haven't been too many stagecoaches rolling through the mountains lately and the warning really wasn't of any more permanent a nature. It was decades later though before Audrain's Lodge was built on the site of the burned-out station.

—JANUARY 23, 1964

GHOSTS IN THE MOUNTAINS

There are ghosts in the Sierra, ghosts along the narrow mountain trails, atop windswept ridges and along the bright streams which pound tortured paths to the valley.

For many years these hills held most of California's people. Few hidden places were not visited at one time or another by the sturdy men who lived in this land and sought a wealth in gold here.

Climbing over smooth rocks in a narrow valley where a mighty river flowed in ages past, we've often wondered how the men who settled a Last Chance or Bedbug Town felt when they beheld a ridge ahead where men had not yet marked it with their civilization.

A wind blows across the ridge, rippling pines in a sea of motion from the height to the valley. It eases the blast from a clear, hot, summer sun. It was the same when California's heart was centered in her mountains. The men who worked, struggled, dreamed of making their fortune and suffered through day after day of backbreaking digging, hauling and seeking must have found some pleasure in a breeze like the one we felt.

Deep in the mountains there's not another soul to be seen. We can walk, climb and gaze for miles without spotting man, woman or child. Yet we know they were here one time, and by the thousands because those men who first worked in these hills left something of themselves behind.

Worn planks show that there could have been a shack beside these sheltered rocks, or those scraps of wood could have been part of a well-used sluice box which may or may not have held sacksful of glittering flakes.

Ancient, metal shoes, which may have been worn by horse or sturdy mule, lie beneath decayed rock and wood, packed into the ground near where they were discarded by a colorful, cursing pack driver with a close schedule to keep.

A piece of shovel or tip from an unrecognizable implement turns up where we'd least expect to find it and we can't help but wonder about the men who used these tools when they were new.

We walk alone hour after hour, through these once populous hills. We're alone only because we came at the wrong time. In another day there would have been many men working to build this flume. Now it is nothing more than a strange trail following the brow of a hill through thick strands of second growth pine whose ancestors were uprooted to make way for an unnatural stream of water.

Not all that the 19th century immigrants left behind added to the beauty of the Sierra or blended with the rugged settings. Man-high tunnels carved through solid rock seem to have little reason for ever having the energy expended on them that their construction must have taken. Then we see the long, curving river bar. A hundred men could have worked claims along the bar once the river was rerouted through the tunnel. Look closely. We can still see picks flashing in the sun, a heavily-bearded young man looking into his first panning for a sight of color. Their ghosts are all through the Sierra.

As evening brings a stronger breeze through the narrow canyon, we can imagine how a lone miner must have stopped work at the close of day to look around these hills and wonder if in a future time anyone would ever find the wealth he discovered here.

—JANUARY 30, 1964

BIDWELL'S GOLD

Gold brought more people to 19th century California than any other single element, but even before the gold rush began a few men realized that California's true wealth lay in her soil.

Sutter was one of the first farmers. He devoted large acres to wheat and cattle. He irrigated with water from the American river, operated a flour mill, sent hunters to the mountains for wild animal skins and had large herds of horses, cows and sheep.

Sutter had a small weaving establishment to produce wool blankets and, realizing that man could not live by bread alone, had a distillery built to convert grain into a palatable liquid potion.

Agriculture was important to the Swiss pioneer who envisioned an empire in the wilderness. To Sutter his farms were also the means of getting him off the hook to the Russians from whom he had purchased livestock, a small launch and the artillery of Fort Ross and Bodega. The wheat which wasn't used to feed his own colony of workers went to the Russians as payment of his debt.

Another early farmer who realized the fertile land could be made to bear huge crops was John Bidwell, who came to California in 1841. Bidwell first worked for Sutter as an early-day farm manager. He helped Sutter keep a daily record of events which has since been published as *Sutter's Diary*.

Bidwell went a step further by becoming an experimenter as well as production farmer. As early as 1847 Bidwell had an orchard on his farm, Rancho Chico. There was at least one planting of each of over 400 different fruit varieties.

He is said to have been father of the raisin industry in his part of the state and was also a pioneer in the manufacture of olive oil. He was an active member and leader in the state agricultural society and always remained close to the land.

In the early 1860's Bidwell planted wine grapes and later hired a wine maker. He raised both Mission and Catawba varieties and would probably have continued wine grape production during his lifetime had he not observed the reaction of workers helping the wine maker. On visiting his wine cellar, Bidwell noticed that the wine maker had an unusually large crew of helpers and that the men appeared unsteady after a few hours on the job.

Bidwell had the grapevines pulled out and smashed barrel after barrel of wine. He was said to have been a great believer in temperance. In 1892 he was Prohibition party candidate for president of the United States.

Bidwell and Sutter both realized that California should build for the future on agriculture despite the fortunes being made in the gold mines.

John Bidwell

Another group which realized the value of California's farmland was the Mormons. Their Salt Lake City of Utah could have been in the Sacramento valley had Brigham Young not feared the dangers of the easy life. Brigham was intelligent enough to know that his "Saints" needed to struggle to stay together and build their new kingdom in the West. He held out for Utah against a large group who had farmed in California and realized its potential for wealth.

There were more men than these few who saw that California would become one of the most fertile and highly productive farmlands of the world, but these were among the first.

—February 6, 1964

EARLY GOLD RUSH DAYS

Henry Bee was a man with a problem. As a minor official in San Jose, Henry knew his duty was to turn 10 Indian prisoners he had captured over to the town alcalde. But there was the problem. The alcalde had rushed off to the gold mines where Henry wanted to be.

The Indians were accused murderers and it wouldn't do to turn them loose in the unprotected village of San Jose. All the able-bodied men had gone to the mines by the middle of June, 1848, and only the women and children were left.

At first few people in San Francisco, Monterey, San Jose or the other small, scattered communities in the state believed the find was of any importance. Sutter and Marshal had originally tried to keep their discovery a secret.

The news leaked out through several sources. When gold was traded for supplies at Brannan and Smith's store in Sacramento, Smith sent word to Brannan in San Francisco. The Mormons working to build the sawmill let the word slip at Coloma and before long the story was spread up and down the state that Marshall had found gold in the tail race of the Coloma sawmill in January, 1848.

A few optimists left for the mountains, but for the most part, the news of a gold strike was received with disbelief. Captain Folsom, quartermaster at San Francisco, said the early flakes he saw were only mica and not gold.

In May, 1848, Bradley, a friend of Folsom's told an acquaintance in Monterey that there was nothing to the story of a gold find on the American river.

On April 15, E. C. Kemble, editor of the *Star*—one of two San Francisco weekly newspapers—announced that he was off to the "rural country," but didn't suggest he would be looking for gold. On May 6, he commented in the *Star* about his trip and praised the scenery, talked about the weather, crops and flowers and mentioned that there was also gold and silver, but didn't make much of the gold strike.

Sam Brannan, always a quick man to scent a profit, made his own visit to the discovery site and returned to San Francisco on May 12 with cans, bottles and leather bags full of gold. Sam convinced the doubters that there might be something to the rumors.

The exodus of San Francisco began. An 1847 census showed 810 people in San Francisco. There were 573 men, 177 women and 60 children. By the middle of June more than three-fourths of the men and many of the women and children had abandoned the town and made for the mountains. The gold rush for the Californians was in full swing, a full season ahead of the rest of the world. Crews abandoned ships, soldiers deserted garrisons and the men sent to bring them back also failed to return. Prisoners slipped away from their jailers and made for the mountains. The jailers set off in hot pursuit and were careful not to find their men.

Sam Brannan

Henry Bee was made of sterner stuff and couldn't allow his Indians to go free. The only solution which came to mind was to take the Indians with him. At the mines Henry put his Indians to work and everybody was happy for awhile.

No matter how good a deal a man might work up through his own initiative, there's always someone to complain and many of the other miners were unhappy with Henry.

They incited his Indians by telling them that they were being exploited and although they had little understanding of whatever that might mean, decided to rebel.

By the time the Indians revolted, Henry had made his fortune and couldn't have cared less. He left his Indians to their own devices, a happy man.

–FEBRUARY 13, 1964

GOLD FEVER IN GRASS VALLEY

Frank Smith was bone tired. It seemed to him as though he'd been walking forever. He had taken nearly five months to travel by wagon train from the Missouri frontier to California in the summer of 1850 and he had been afoot most of the way.

He'd gone upriver from Sacramento to Marysville by steamer and outfitted there for his first try at gold mining. Striking out east and then north from Marysville, Frank shuffled up one dusty hill and then down its opposite side and up another, always climbing higher toward the mountains.

On his back were nearly 50 pounds of provisions including two wool blankets, a week's supply of pork and hard bread, a pick, pan and shovel plus rifle and ammunition.

The pack was an unaccustomed and cumbersome weight which wouldn't sit right. It poked into the small of his back and sent a dull pain through all his body. After awhile he jiggled the weight higher on his shoulders, but it kept settling into the same tender part of his back until he came to accept the pain.

Leather pack straps wore at his shoulders until he was sure that his skin was cut through. Frank's rest stops came around more often as he slowly dragged his way through the day. The hot sun baked his back and brought out sweat which chilled him whenever he stopped walking. He had to keep moving. Thoughts of a rich gold find kept pushing him on. There was also the knowledge that others had been this way before. That thought gnawed at his pride until he knew that he couldn't turn back. What one man could do, so also could he do, and on he plodded through dust whirls and dry, burnt-grass country.

Frank camped at a stream that first night, but had no desire to try his newly purchased gold pan. He lacked the strength or interest to kindle a fire and settled for a few dry mouths-full of hard bread.

During his trek across the dusty foothills, Frank had considered discarding a blanket. He reasoned that a country as hot as he'd been

through couldn't be too cold at night, but when he tried to sleep, he wished for at least two more heavy blankets.

It took him three more days before he felt he was deep enough in the mountains to begin mining. Frank had already walked over millions of dollars in gold ore on his way to the Feather River country, but had no idea of the wealth underfoot.

His first mining camp was in Grass Valley on the south fork of the Feather. This spot later became known as Little Grass Valley and is today buried under Little Grass Valley Lake.

There were many brush and cloth covered tents in the valley and Frank soon joined a company of men on their way to the middle fork of the Feather where prospects were thought to be better. On Onion Valley Creek which feeds into the middle fork, the group extended their credit to the breaking point to build a diversion dam above a likely-looking bend in the creek.

Once completed they sifted through cubic yard after yard of creek bottom to recover no more than a few dollars in gold. The company quietly disbanded and the mountain merchants who had supplied credit for the undertaking wrote off their loss as a hazard of mountain store-keeping.

With winter coming on Frank started back toward the Sacramento Valley to try his hand at foothill mining, confident that next summer, when he returned to the middle fork, he'd know better where to prospect.

(Frank Smith is not a literal character, but a composite of many miners of the early 1850's who struggled in the Sierra gold fields.)

–FEBRUARY 20, 1964

SIERRA GAMBLERS

Dry California summers greatly helped commerce in the Sierra mining camps the first years after the gold strike. The warm days from May to September when there is little or no rain allowed storekeepers to safely open shop with little more protection than a cloth roof.

An early writer of the mining days describes a store located at the mouth of Nelson Creek along the Middle Fork of the Feather River. Trees were cut nearby and hauled to the site for a pole frame. Cloth was then stretched over the frame to make a roof. Branches and brush were piled on the sides as walls.

For fixtures large trees were cut to length, split and smoothed with an axe, adz or whatever other finishing tools the storekeeper might own. These hewn slabs then become counter tops, shelves, tables and stool tops. Kegs formed the legs of the counter. It was said that a half day's work was usually enough to make a counter or table top.

Once the fixtures were installed all that remained was to stock the store with brandy, whisky and tobacco first of all, and then some of the more substantial foodstuffs. The storekeeper always stocked a large supply of cards for the game of euchre or poker—favorites of the miners.

Few prospectors carried more supplies to the mines than they could pack in on their backs. They had no desire to load a mule with supplies for once at the mines, they would have little use for the mule and didn't want to bother with his care.

The store at Nelson Creek was undoubtedly supplied by mule train since it was several years before there were wagon roads beyond Onion Valley. Only the mules, oftentimes as many as 100 to a string, could make their way over the high ridges and to the camps in the steep canyons. To reach the Middle Fork from Onion Valley a zigzag path was cut from bench to bench down the side of the mountain. A few animals were lost now and then as they missed their footing and were unable to regain their balance with barrels of flour, pork liquor, bags of beans or boxes and bales of miscellaneous merchandise strapped to their backs.

To the store or tent tavern came the itinerant gambler who would stop over at a camp only long enough to clean out the easy money or lose his own poke.

Sierra gamblers followed a technique which had already been perfected in nature. They adopted protective coloration in the mining camps and dressed like the miners they were out to fleece. Hats were the rounded, low crowned felts and shirts were of flannel although a gambler's trousers were generally in better repair and less grease stained than the typical miner's.

A gambler's hands generally were more delicate, much less calloused, and for some unknown reason most of the gamblers were smooth shaven while the miners had either mustache, beard or both.

The early gamblers were said to have been men of heart who after cleaning out a miner would often stake the man to enough for his next meal and not leave a victim entirely destitute nor desert a sick comrade.

Storekeepers or saloon owners were promptly paid by the gambler for use of the facilities and the man would be on his way after a day or two of play in any one camp.

In the early years nearly everyone in the land of plenty remained a gentleman above all else, but once it became a case of hard scrabble to make even a day's wages in the gold fields, there became fewer and fewer gentlemen.

–FEBRUARY 27, 1964

THE RAREST SIGHT OF ALL

"Drop your pick and come a-runnin'. It's the biggest find since that 20 pound nugget at Oddie's Bar." Long John Tate went racing through the camp, shouting at the top of his lungs until all the miners at Last Chance gathered 'round to see what the excitement was all about.

Long John could hardly talk. He was out of breath from racing through the camp, halloing-up the miners. John Tate was normally a quiet enough sort and the only time anyone had ever seen him this excited before was when he'd panned two tin cupsfull of gold in a single day.

"Come on and tell us," shouted a bearded, gaunt-faced young man. "Who made the discovery and are there still claims enough left for all of us?"

"It's not gold, you poor mistaken excuse for a man," John yelled back. "It's better than that. It's a woman. A real live one and she's over at No Ear Bar. I ain't seen her, but sure 'nough talked to a fellow that did. And she's there alright."

The year was 1851 in the Feather River country and women were more than rare among the deep canyons. It was as though there had never been such a thing as an opposite sex.

Most of the miners in the camps were young men and many of them had been away from home for two and three years. They had left mothers, sisters and sweethearts behind and not seen many women since reaching California. Some of the pre-gold rush settlers had families in California, but few of these women went to the rugged Feather River country with their men.

For many of the miners who stayed through the winter in their deep canyon camps had their last look at a touch of femininity in Sacramento or Marysville.

The Last Chance miners knew why Long John Tate hadn't ventured off alone to view this most rare of all rare sights. Being away from female companionship they felt as he did. Any one of them would have been too embarrassed to have sought out the lady on his own, but together the men gathered their group courage about them as a protective cloak.

Faces were hurriedly washed. Their best flannel shirts and least-patched trousers were hauled from the bottom of pack bags. The low crowned, round miners' hats were dusted off with flourishes and the entire camp set off for No Ear Bar.

They were little more than three miles away from the camp where this sample of the fair sex was said to be, but the first mile was straight downhill to the Middle Fork canyon and then upstream over rock slides and through ragged, jumbled country which would have been an obstacle to a young mountain goat. The creek had to be forded a number of times before they reached No Ear Bar, but the trip was well worth while.

The lady's husband, having been alone in the mountains for two seasons, knew the loneliness of his fellow miners and graciously presented his wife to the Last Chancers. Most of the men were too tongue-tied to mumble more than a "Pleased to meet you, ma'am," but their eyes spoke volumes.

The way back seemed faster to the men for they talked of nothing but the beautiful creature they'd been lucky enough to see. Even the steep, uphill ascent was a snap to men who learned that there really were still women in the world.

The instance wasn't an isolated one in the early years. Story after story is told of entire camps traveling all day just to catch sight of a woman. But then scarcity often plays a part in the values of men.

—March 5, 1964

FIRE PREVENTION

"Who's been stealing all the fire buckets off Main street?" E. B. Boust, editor and publisher of the Weekly Patriot in Iowa Hill, was more than a little disturbed by the thievery of fire fighting buckets from the Main street tanks.

Being a tactful sort, the editor remarked that the buckets were "mysteriously disappearing." He didn't name names or come right out and charge the citizens of the community with disregard for their own safety, but he did make some strong hints in his issue of January 15, 1859.

The buckets were part of the town's insurance against another catastrophe like the fire of February, 1857, when the Placer County community was burned to the ground.

Iowa Hill had become a town in the spring of 1854 with the discovery of several placer claims nearby. It prospered from a simple camp to a fairly sizeable community with many stores including a livery stable, drugstore, hardware, mercantile establishment and several saloons, including the popular Bed Rock Saloon.

After the fire of '57, Iowa Hill was rebuilt on grander proportions than before. To guarantee that fire would never again be the serious threat it had that spring day of '57, precautions were taken. Store owners built ladders which they attached to their store fronts in order that fire fighters could extinguish small sparks before they became uncontrollable flames.

There were a number of water tanks installed on the town's only business street and water buckets were cached carefully away beside the water tanks. The idea was a good one, but the buckets were just the kind a housewife might need to carry water from well to house, or the kind a miner might use to carry gravel or haul water to his rocker where he washed gold. It was more than could be expected that the buckets would stay in place. The good newspaper editor should have known better than to have gone against human nature. Better that he suggested the town apply for government aid to secure an unlimited free supply of buckets.

Fire was an ever present danger in all the camps. Another "good one" nearly started in Iowa Hill the night a disgruntled miner lost his temper and his money gambling. He actually lost his money first. The temper followed immediately thereafter. He took his last quarter and heaved it at a glass camphene lamp. Luckily, the quarter broke the glass bottom of the lamp in such a way that the camphene oil streamed out without igniting. There was a mad dash for cover at first until the men saw that no damage was done. They derided their companion for being a poor sport and suggested he had better stay away from such exhilarating pursuits until he learned to better control his steam.

Wooden construction, open fires and haphazard stove pipes all contributed to the fire danger. Editor Boust who was never short on suggestions recommended that a stovepipe committee be formed to check every house in town and warn guilty ones if their pipes needed tending.

All these factors added to the fire danger, but the biggest problem was water. January 1859 was a dry month. There had been fog in the Sacramento valley and the Placer County foothills where Iowa Hill was located, but the fog failed to condense into enough moisture for miners to work or for fire fighters to battle blazes. It was a season of caution for the Iowans on their Hill.

–MARCH 12, 1964

THE VALLEY INDIANS

November sunshine filtered through valley oaks on two Indian squaws intent on their acorn gathering. As far as they knew there wasn't another human in the grove. There were lots of acorns and gathering them was a simple task. The women worked slowly, piling acorns into conical, wicker baskets.

A noise from behind a bush startled the Indians and they paused, listened an instant, turned slowly and spotted two white men coming toward them. Like frightened deer the women bounded through the woods, leaving their day's collection of acorns behind.

"Those two must be the ugliest females in the whole world," one of the men said to his partner. "I've seen Indians and more Indians, but that must be about as low as they ever get."

He was right. The valley Indians were one of the most basic races on earth. Life for them was eating, sleeping, gathering acorns for flour, collecting insects for food and hunting a few of the easier to catch animals. Left alone they might have developed a higher form of culture or they might have continued their easy life of taking what the land had to offer and living each day as it came.

E. Gould Buffum was one of the two men who had spotted the women. The miners had watched the scantily clad Indians for awhile before stepping forth from hiding.

The women were naked except for a sorry coyote skin which hung from waist to knees. It was a costume that could have been the stuff from which men's dreams are made. On an island beauty or fiction-type Indian maiden it would have been enough to have driven most men to distraction, but on these two distant cousins of the human race it was less than appealing.

Buffum had been a newspaperman in the East before joining the militia for California service. He'd served nearly three years in California and set out to become a miner upon his discharge in 1848. He traveled from his Los Angeles post to Sacramento and had left Sacramento

November 16, 1848, with five other discharged militiamen, bound for the mountains.

After becoming lost in the hills, the men finally located Johnson's ranch on Bear River, southeast of Marysville. Camped near the ranch, Buffum and a partner had come across the Indians.

They observed that the women's heads were completely shaved and covered with a black, tarry paint. The same paint was used with great gusto on their faces where military-like whiskers were painted. Only another Indian of the same tribe could have appreciated such beauty.

Buffum and his partner followed the women to a village of about 20 circular wigwams located on both sides of a ravine. The wigwams were of brush, plastered with mud and the miners later learned that each one housed three or four Indians.

One member of the tribe spoke Spanish and Buffum was able to carry on a conversation with him. He noted that all the men of the tribe were entirely nude, but failed to mention if they shaved and painted their heads as did the women.

Questioning the Spanish-speaking Indian, the men learned that gold was nothing new to the tribe. Their interpreter said that he had often seen it in the rivers. A tribe living one step from starvation had little use for the bright metal which made neither good arrow points nor any needed utensils. The white men who set such great store by the "worthless yellow rocks" must have been as strange to the redmen as they were to the gold seekers.

–MARCH 19, 1964

POKER FLAT JUSTICE

It was going to be a lonely Christmas for Burke without his partner, Lyons. But then it was his own fault. Burke had stabbed Lyons to death just five days before Christmas at Paddy's Goose, a saloon in Poker Flat.

Burke and Lyons had joined forces at Poker Flat in September, 1858. They rarely argued although Lyons had been known to lose his temper on occasion.

On December 20 the partners washed up after a day spent working their claim. It was a Monday evening and after a rip-roaring Sunday, the pair weren't in much of a mood to settle down to a back breaking week's work.

"Let's go down to Paddy's for a few drinks and supper, Burke," Lyons suggested. "I don't want to waste the evening cooking and cleaning pots and dishes."

"That's a good idea," Burke had responded. He shared his partner's aversion to kitchen drudgery.

Lyons bought a pair of drinks and then Burke bought. It was their usual way of sharing work and expenses. After more than a few rounds, the men staggered back to a larger room where they muddled through a heavy dinner, washed down with a few more swallows of liquor.

Lyons abruptly lurched to his feet and angled toward the door, mumbling something about a breath of air. Burke sat alone and listless in the room, staring at his plate, then fumbled for another drink.

In a short time, Lyons burst back in complaining, "Awright Burke, where's my pipe? You've had your eyes on it for a week and now you've stolen it from me. Won't do you a bit of good. I know you've got it. You're the only one who could have. Get to your feet, man, and give me that pipe."

Lyons tugged at his friend, lost his footing and crashed into the table, toppling onto Burke. They rolled on the floor for a few minutes, then a knife flashed, plunged and plunged again. Lyons was dying and Burke was covered with gore.

Sounds of the struggle brought a handful of miners from the bar. Burke was held, his knife taken and a call sent out to assemble a miner's jury.

It wasn't long before 82 miners gathered to hear Burke's testimony. Justice Fitzgerald tallied votes after all the evidence was heard and the men had time to consider the known facts. The count was 40 to

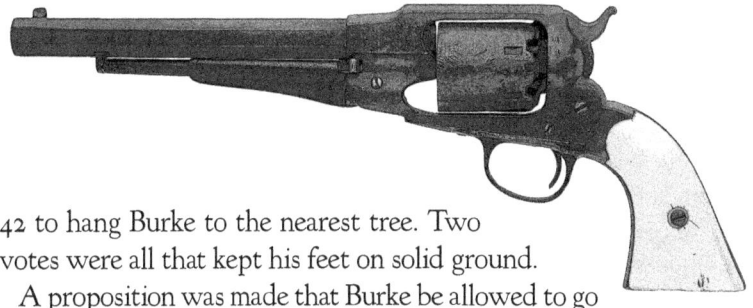

42 to hang Burke to the nearest tree. Two votes were all that kept his feet on solid ground.

A proposition was made that Burke be allowed to go free. He would be given $25 and two revolvers if he would leave Poker Flat that night. Burke realized that his chances for survival would be slim. With 40 men eager to hang him, the accused knew that he would not get far from Poker Flat.

Burke argued that he should get a regular trial where he'd have a chance of enjoying his freedom if found innocent and would at least know how he were going to die if found guilty.

Taken to Pine Grove the prisoner again told of his fight with Lyons, but revealed, this time, that he had purchased the fatal weapon at a butcher shop just two hours before the stabbing. Such knives were common tools in the mines and this wasn't enough to make a case against the man. Also, there were witnesses who had heard a quarrel. There had been a fight and it could only be assumed Burke was smart enough not to have planned a murder in a place like Paddy's Goose where he could have easily been discovered.

Burke was set free for lack of sufficient evidence to prove his guilt, and as he left the courtroom puffing slowly on Lyons' pipe he thought what a lonely Christmas season it was without his partner.

–MARCH 26, 1964

DAY TO DAY LIVING IN PLACER COUNTY

Fred Blume was happy to be alive and walking about naturally after his mining accident. A big raffle was planned at the Bed Rock saloon and Druggist W. B. Lyon was prepared to offer free medical advice to his customers. Not much out of the ordinary was taking place in Iowa Hill, Placer County, during the first part of the year 1859.

On New Year's Day some exceedingly rich quartz ore specimens were taken from the Lebanon tunnel on Prospect Hill. A Mr. Huff on Elizabeth Hill had panned out $33 worth of gold in two pan-flings, working during a severe storm. The winter of 1858-59 had been a dry one and Huff took advantage of the rainfall which furnished enough water for him to pan gold.

Six or eight robbers—witnesses couldn't agree—took $2200 from the Wells Fargo treasure box on the Forest Hill stage on a Tuesday morning, January 11. This stage, which connected with the Yankee Jim coach at Smith's ranch bound for Auburn, was understandably late.

Reports came in that 40 Indians were killed in Round Valley, Mendocino County, on New Year's Day. The Indians were said to have been stealing livestock and killing hogs. At least 170 Indians had been killed in this area from December 1 through January 1.

Fred Blume had been working in the Pioneer tunnel at Roach Hill on November 3 when his mining accident occurred. A large bank of sand had caved in on him, dislocating his back and causing other minor injuries. Blume, in an advertisement in the Iowa Hill WEEKLY PATRIOT of January 15, 1859, claimed he owed his life to skillful attention from Dr. G. M. Sheridan. The doctor had treated Blume after the cave-in and Fred said that he was again able to walk erect and was not deformed.

"I am still weak, but with the help of God will soon be able to handle a pick and shovel and put in as hard licks as I ever did before," Blume stated. Incidentally, he recommended Dr. Sheridan to all his brother miners and to all persons requiring aid of a skillful physician and surgeon.

Advertising has come a long way since those days and doctors now must find some more subtle way of securing patients. Druggists no longer advertise as Lyon did that he would give free advice. Today they stress their ability to accurately compound prescriptions, using highest quality compounds. Raffles such as that at the Bed Rock are still carried on, but not legally. Newspapers are restricted from carrying advertising of raffles and could never be as open as the *Weekly Patriot* was.

The Bed Rock proprietor announced that a large, fine music box in good order, a fine Colt revolver in good order and silver watch—that's right, it was in good order too—would be the prizes. Tickets were $1 each. One hundred were to be sold and the drawing would be held when the "tickets were sold out." The raffle business was good. The following week's paper announced that the drawing would be held the next day.

The beginning of the first California Grade A dairy was forecast in another ad run in the *Weekly Patriot*. J. Hart claimed to have fresh, pure milk for sale which he was willing to deliver at reasonable rates. He concluded with the notation that, "No stump-tail cows milked." And thus quality became an early ingredient of California dairy products.

Such were the trifles which made up day to day living in Placer County during 1858-59.

—APRIL 2, 1964

CIVIL WAR POLITICS

A federal Conscription Act of 1863, passed to raise an army for the North during the Civil War, was never used in California. It wasn't that Californians were so patriotic that they volunteered in large numbers. That wasn't it at all. There were too many Southerners in the state and the boys were needed at home.

California had been strongly Democratic before the election of Abraham Lincoln, a Republican. In 1859 the pro-slavery Democrats held major state offices. By the following year there was a slight change in sentiment, enough for Lincoln to lead in California by a bare 1,000 votes during the presidential election,

When the state legislature convened in Sacramento on January 7, 1861, there were 18 Northern senators and 15 Southern. Northerners held the balance of power in the assembly with 40 against 29 Southern-born members.

Senator Gwin who had served California since 1850 was known to be a strong Southern sympathizer. The legislature replaced him in March, 1861, by selecting John McDougal, an anti-secessionist, to represent California in Washington, D.C. The Northern cause appeared to be gaining strength.

Suggestions had been voiced that California start its own Pacific Republic should the North and South go to war. Sentiment was strong for an independent nation in the West with California its hub, but largely through the efforts of Thomas Starr King, California remained in the union. King was a New Englander who had come to

Senator Gwin

San Francisco in 1860, served as a minister and traveled the state, forcefully speaking against secession.

By the September elections of 1861 there were four factions battling for California votes. Republicans placed Leland Stanford on the ballot for governor; Southern Democrats nominated J. R. McConnell and both the Union party and Northern Democrats backed John Conness.

On election day there were riots at the polls as bitter feelings flushed to the surface. Voters showed that they were opposed to secession and to slavery by electing Stanford in a landslide.

When word was received that Fort Sumter had been fired upon, requests were made for infantry and cavalry volunteers. Four regiments of infantry and one of cavalry were quickly raised, but these men weren't sent East to fight. They were stationed throughout California in locations where secessionist uprisings were expected. Most of the troops were sent to Southern California and some on to Yuma, Arizona.

Thomas Starr King

Later requests raised the enlistments, but again these men served in California and the West, battling more Indians than Johnny Rebs.

It was believed that about one-third of the Californians were Southern sympathizers in 1863 and for that reason the federal Conscription Act was never used. It was felt, as we mentioned, that if too many troops were drawn away, California could easily be won by the Confederacy.

The Knights of the Golden Circle and King of the Columbia Star, two secret organizations, were said to have trained men ready to help a Southern army should one enter California.

It was touch and go for many years whether the state would stay with the North, but the majority opinion backed by a strong volunteer force held California.

–April 17, 1964

DAMMING THE YUBA RIVER

Campers, water skiers and fishermen today flock to Bullard's Bar Reservoir in Yuba county, but no matter how many visit here, their number is still far below the 19th century population.

Present day visitors see few signs to tell them this was a large population center nor do most know of the suffering and heartbreak associated with this locale.

It started with a shipwreck. Dr. Bullard for whom the camp was named had no intention of making California his home, but was instead bound for the Sandwich Islands (Hawaiian Islands). He had left Brooklyn, N.Y., but was shipwrecked off the California coast and settled here.

When he learned of the gold strike, Dr. Bullard staked a claim along the North Yuba and was soon followed by other miners. Camps became so numerous along the Yuba in 1850 that it is said a message could be sent by word of mouth from Downieville all the way to Marysville. Sounds like a good way to beat the high costs of mail service, although a bit public.

Above Bullard's and today buried under the lake's water behind Bullard's Bar Dam was Foster's Bar. Founder of this community was William M. Foster, a survivor of the Donner party tragedy. At Foster's there were 1500 voters in 1850 and possibly many more who failed to be counted at the polls.

Tragedy was the start of both camps and at Bullard's Bar it continued, at least for the early bridge builders. A bridge was built across the Yuba as early as 1850. The first one washed away the following spring. Each year efforts were made to build a substantial enough bridge to withstand the annual floods caused by heavy rainfall and snowpack melt. Each year a bridge was built and each spring one was washed away.

In 1858 George Mix invested $7,000 to build a bridge which could withstand a normal Yuba flood. The bridge held out the first season

Bullard's Bar Dam

and then another. There was hope that the Yuba had been thwarted. After another successful season the Yuba miners became smug, but the flood of 1862 wiped away every last trace of their smiles. Mix's bridge was carried downstream and smashed by the rampaging river.

Later another bridge was built, this one upstream of the former attempts. It stood until 1875 before being torn loose and washed downstream. John Ramm doubled Mix's investment and spent $15,000 on a subsequent bridge which lasted through nature's violence, but succumbed to man. Floods had no part in its undoing. Progress marked the last chapter on the bridge building efforts as well as on the fate of Bullard's, Foster's and the many other camps upstream from Bullard's. Water, as deep as 100 feet, now covers these once-busy gold mining camps.

In place of the bridges, today stands Bullard's Bar Dam with a narrow, but colorful highway which winds through the foothills, crosses the dam, meanders past the reservoir and then climbs up into the hills.

Foster and Bullard built solid communities from their tragedies, but eventually succumbed to changes called for by a 20th century civilization.

–April 9, 1964

CROSSING DEATH VALLEY

William Manley had always led a decent enough life and that was what made him wonder how he'd ever strayed onto this path which surely led to the depths of hell.

Manley and his party were in Death Valley, far off the track to the gold fields—their destination that winter of 1849.

There had been seven eager, young men who left Salt Lake for California in November, 1849. Manley was chosen to be leader of the group and the Colorado River was to be their path to California and the gold fields.

At the Colorado they built a small boat and set out downstream, not realizing this river was unlike any they'd ever known in their eastern homeland. The men had not gotten far when their boat was smashed onto rocks and swamped. They were splashed into the roiling stream. Fighting to get ashore they saw their boat battered to bits and felt lucky to have escaped alive.

Bedraggled, miserable, minus supplies and with hopes of besting the river gone, Manley directed their march back to Salt Lake. On the way they met a large party of California-bound migrants. There were at least 100 wagons.

Some of this party joined the seven and furnished supplies to help them. They agreed that the quickest route to California was due west.

Along the way they were joined by a small party from Illinois. None of the group had a definite plan. They were willing to be guided by anyone with a plausible idea on how they might reach California, and reach it before the gold was all gone.

They struggled across the barren country thinking the land was bound to change. They were well into Death Valley when the realization came that the only change would be for the worse. Water was scarce and food supplies were soon at the dangerous level. Not a game animal stirred. Had it been any other season than winter the party would have slowly dried out, one by one, and fried to a crisp.

Manley and another young man left to seek help. The two young men crossed the valley and desert beyond, reaching San Francisco where they were able to get supplies and horses.

Manley and his partner were gone a month and in that time a number of those in Death Valley died. One small group of men left the main party and attempted to find, on their own, a short way across the valley. On the Mojave Desert one man died and then two more a short distance from the first. Nothing was heard of the others, but seven years later the bones of nine men were found on the desert and it is believed they were the missing members.

With fresh supplies, horses to carry those who couldn't walk and Manley's guidance in following the trail, survivors made their way safely out of Death Valley and on across the desert. They reached Los Angeles in March, 1850.

The shortcut to California cost five months time, many lives and the realization that the goal is sometimes not worth the pursuit.

–April 23, 1964

THE COFFEE POT BOMBARDMENT

The year was 1846. In June the rash Bear Flag revolt showed Mexico that the Americans intended to take and fight to keep California.

On July 7 the flag was raised over Monterey and two days later over San Francisco or "Yerba Buena" as it was then called. With a small man in charge of a big job—commander of American military forces at Yerba Buena—any minor incident could have been blown out of all proportions, and was.

Captain Joseph B. Hull of the sloop-of-war *Warren* was the commander and according to some observers of that time was a man inclined to be "over particular and fussy, a man of small mind."

Colonel Mariano Vallejo who had been a staunch friend of the Americans and one who actually favored acquisition of California by the United States, was imprisoned at Sutter's Fort. Native Californians suffered raids upon their livestock and other property by the U.S. military authorities. The natives were ripe for revolt against the Americans.

With this setting of unrest, taut nerves and general knowledge that a fight could start anytime, a bit of comic opera relief gave everyone a chance to let off steam.

Colonel Mariano Vallejo

Captain King and his Kanaka steward started the fuss with their fancy coffee pot. It was a beautiful, gleaming machine which would be appreciated today by any coffee connoisseur who believes there's a better way to make his favorite brew.

King's device held about a gallon and a half and worked similarly to a pressure cooker. It had been brought from the Sandwich (Hawaiian) Islands by King to California. Both he and his steward had mastered the machine and were able to safely turn out a respectable cup of coffee.

The secret was to adjust a screw-valve to permit just enough steam to escape, but not too much. Having other jobs to do in the kitchen of Brown's Hotel one evening, the steward left the marvelous coffee maker in charge of a second cook who failed to understand the principle of the pot or the danger of trapped steam.

Seeing what he thought to be too much steam escaping, the novice closed the screw-valve as tightly as he could. When enough pressure built up there was only one possibility. It happened just as James Watt, the Scottish steam pioneer, would have predicted. There was a shattering explosion.

The cook was thrown 20 yards from his kitchen; stools flew, kitchen utensils banged, clattered and smashed about the small room.

Captain Hull, the brave defender of Yerba Buena whose headquarters were in the same hotel, didn't wait to check the facts. He knew there had been a bombardment and off he raced for the barracks which, at that time, were in the old Custom House.

"Sound the long roll. Muster the men. Look lively there. We're under attack. The Spaniards have come to take the city and we'll all be cut to ribbons unless we form our defenses."

Captain Hull was indeed a decisive man and a thorough one. He sent soldiers racing through the city to gather the few hundred citizens together. They were formed into loose ranks and ready to fire whenever the brave captain gave the word.

Marines were sent out as scouts to determine the enemy's strength. Signal flares flashed from shore to Captain Hull's sailors aboard ship. They were ordered to stand by until needed.

What a battle it would have been if the good captain had only found an enemy. The matter was cleared up after it finally became apparent that there was no invading army.

Nearly everyone had a good laugh over the "Coffee Pot Bombardment." The only two who weren't laughing were Captain Hull and the second cook. Humiliation consumed the captain while the cook resolved to seek a job safer than coffee pot tender.

–April 30, 1964

JUSTICE IN SUTTER'S FORT

If it was all right for California women to smoke at bullfights, executions and funerals, there was no reason why smoking shouldn't be allowed during a criminal trial. Sam Brannon, a reformed Mormon serving as judge at the first Sutter's Fort trial, made the ruling in the winter of 1848.

There was no question raised about the brandy which sat on a table next to a pitcher of water. In fact the water was hardly touched during the trial. Judge, jury, prisoner and spectators all favored the taste and didn't consider for an instant its necessity during the criminal proceedings.

The trial started because C. E. Pickett, a storekeeper at Sutter's Fort, poured two barrels of buckshot into a fellow merchant, Isaac W. Alderman, a reportedly "mean sort of fellow" who had migrated to Sutter's from Oregon. Alderman was said to have killed two men in Oregon and would probably have made Pickett his first California victim if Pickett had not shot first.

Trouble started when Alderman attempted to use a portion of Pickett's rented store space for his own. The alcalde ruled that Alderman was out of order, but he persisted and Pickett gained another favorable decision from the alcalde.

The Oregonian was a firm believer in taking what he wanted and bullying those who opposed him. He took up an axe and sought to scare Pickett into granting him the extra space he sought, but Pickett held his ground, shotgun cocked and ready to fire.

Alderman made a fatal mistake of underestimating his man and kept advancing until Pickett let fly with both barrels of buckshot. Adlerman was dead in short order.

The alcalde had been a business partner of the deceased and delegated authority to his assistant who resigned, leaving no one to try the case. Brannan who also operated a store at Sutter's was prevailed upon to serve as alcalde.

Sutter's Fort

Sam Brannan was never a man to miss an opportunity and possibly deciding that here might be a way to get rid of two competitors at once, agreed to serve not only as judge, but as prosecutor.

Once the details of the trial were settled upon and it was ruled that there was precedence for smoking since California women indulged at public gatherings, Brannan made his plea as prosecutor. Pickett then had his chance at rebuttal.

When one of Pickett's witnesses had finished testifying to Alderman's bad character, Sutter, who was a member of the jury rose and announced, "Gentlemen, the man is dead. I won't sit here any longer and listen to such things being said about him." He started to leave the courtroom, but was prevailed upon to remain and serve out his duty as juror. There is speculation that he took a sip from his jug and dozed off in a happy, righteous state of mind.

After the first day of trial there was no way of holding the prisoner in confinement and he was allowed to take his revolver and knife from the table where they were being held and march off to his own quarters.

Jurors got together the next day, had a few glasses of brandy to clear the cobwebs from their minds and deliberated. The result was a hung jury. Four were for acquittal, three for manslaughter and five for willful murder. At a second trial, Pickett was acquitted and allowed to return to store-keeping.

Looking back through the years the trial appears to have been more of a comedy than a search for justice and could well have been recognized as such at that time, at least to all but the accused.

–May 7, 1964

DOÑA'S PROMISE

The Russian nobleman stared hard at the fading California shoreline. His face was set, stern looking, masking the strong emotions which churned inside.

On shore watching the departure was the woman he loved, a Californian beauty whom he had known for six short weeks. The pair had sworn their undying love and Nikolai Rezanof, the Russian, had vowed he would return to claim his bride.

Rezanof was commander of the Russian ship *Juno* which sailed into San Francisco bay in 1806. His ship was first of the Russian vessels which came to the new world with intentions of establishing trade and perhaps occupying California as a Russian colony.

At first the Russians had been wary and anchored out of reach of the guns from Fort San Joaquin of San Francisco. But their fears were soon dispelled by the friendly greeting they received from Jose Dario Arguello, commander of the port. Rezanof and his crew were warmly welcomed by the Californians and found the new land to their liking.

Doña Concepcion, the lovely, 17-year-old daughter of the port commander was immediately taken by the handsome nobleman. The Russian, being a normal, young male and, in addition, one who had been at sea for many months, found the señorita charming.

In the brief time that Rezanof's ship was in port, the Russian and beautiful señorita came to fall in love. It was a very proper affair, complete with chaperone, but even so the young couple found enough time alone to talk and plan for the future, a future together.

Rezanof delayed the *Juno*'s departure as long as he could, but when the hour came told Doña again and again that he would return for her. She promised to wait and be true to him and would live only for his return.

Six years passed, long years for Doña, before any Russians returned and then it was a group who founded Fort Ross on the north coast. Rezanof was not with this group and it was not until 30 years after his departure from California that Doña Concepcion learned her lover had died in Siberia shortly after his return home.

Nikolai Petrovich Rezanov

The Spanish beauty was no longer a beauty. A lifetime of waiting had taken its toll. Through all those years she remained true to her word and never married.

Doña entered the convent at Benicia and kept her vow to the Russian. She became Sister Mary Dominica Arguello, the first native daughter to receive the Dominican habit in California.

She lived at the convent until her death on December 23, 1857. A plaque on her grave notes the distinction of being first native-born Dominican sister in California.

Rezanof could have sailed back to Russia with Doña in 1806 or jumped ship and lived with her in the land of milk and honey. If he had done either they might possibly have lived happily ever after, but odds are against it, and this may have been, after all, a happy ending.

–May 15, 1964

MULE TRADING

Missouri mule traders, noted for the great endurance of their animals during the time when mule power was important, very likely got their stock from California.

The first overland traders came to California in 1829 from Santa Fe and Taos, New Mexico. The trip of some 1200 miles took from four to five months each way, and the traders brought serapes, woolen and cotton goods, blankets and whisky to trade for California horses and mules.

A later overland trader from New Mexico was David E. Jackson who arrived in Los Angeles in December, 1831, with a party of 10 men, one a Negro slave. Jackson carried Mexican silver to pay for the 600 mules and 100 horses he purchased.

He traveled as far north as San Francisco and spent four months in the state, collecting the large herd which he sold in New Mexico and Missouri.

Business flourished for the traders who braved the hot, southern, desert route, fought off Indians and opened traffic to, and trade with, California.

Jacob P. Leese, more enterprising than his fellow traders, determined

Wild Mule

to corner the mule market by making contact with the Mexican governor, José Figueroa, at Monterey. Figueroa was interested in trade and commerce and agreed that Leese could operate throughout California, buying mules through the missions.

Leese had arrived in California in 1833 and stayed until September, 1834, making contacts with the missions and arranging for exclusive buying rights. He started back to New Mexico with a herd of 450 mules and high hopes for a profitable business venture.

The mule trader's plan ended in disaster when Indians attacked his party along the Mojave River in southeastern California. Every animal was driven off and the "king of the mule traders" lost his golden opportunity.

This lucrative livestock business was made possible by the first Spanish soldier to lead a party overland into California, Juan Bautista de Anza. The soldier led a small group from Mexico to as far north as Monterey in 1774. Proving his ability to make the rough trip through harsh country, de Anza was sent again to California from Mexico in 1776 with colonists—many of them women and children—supplies and large herds of fine horses and mules.

Years later de Anza was probably cursed by Mexican ranchers who saw wild bands of horses and mules cut up their valuable pasture land, reducing grazing for cattle. For many years the wild stock was hunted and shot since they had no value. When traders created a market for California horses and mules in Missouri and other states, hunting parties sought the animals for their sale value.

De Anza must surely have brought asses or donkeys to California since the mule herds did increase through the years and it is unlikely that there were donkeys in California before his journeys. The male ass and fine Spanish mares bred to produce a sturdy mule which finally came to be in demand for hauling heavy wagons over mountains and through deserts.

At the time of the California gold rush, mules reared in California were sold in Missouri to emigrant parties and turned back again toward their homeland. With such a roundabout way of getting back where they started from, it's no wonder mules came to be noted for their obstinacy.

–May 21, 1964

A CASE OF BAD TIMING

John Turner whistled happily as he shoveled gravel into the sluice box at his Yuba River claim. In two weeks John was leaving the mountains for Sacramento and then back home to Missouri.

He was one of the early immigrants to California during the first days of the gold rush and had been lucky. His first claim had yielded several thousand dollars in gold and John had been fortunate enough to stake other profitable diggings.

In Missouri a wife and young son waited for him. The boy had been thought too young to make the California trip and John was confident he would make enough in a season to return for them. Besides there was his family in Missouri who would look after his wife and son.

"It's a beautiful country and this is where we're going to settle," he thought to himself as he worked in the hot sun along the cool, deep Yuba River. "There's room here to grow, hills and mountains and a lot of land waiting for the plow. I may even open a store with all this money I've saved. We'll live like folks was meant to live."

John was an industrious worker, stayed away from the gambling and saloon tent at the meager camp downriver and bought only a bare necessity of supplies. He had few friends, but liked everyone he met. He just didn't have the time to make friends. John was only interested in accumulating enough money to get a good start in life for himself and his young family.

Two miles upriver was Lon Crane who had worked as hard as John, but not been as fortunate. Claim after claim proved unprofitable and the blazing sun pouring down on him was only a curse. Lon came to hate the mountains which sapped the strength of a downhearted man. The Yuba claim he worked was to be his last before he returned to his eastern home.

While John worked and sang, pouring shovel after shovel of gravel into his sluice box and plucking out flakes of fine gold, Lon received

bad news. A letter brought upriver by a friend told him that the girl who was waiting back home had decided to quit waiting. By the time Lon got the letter, she had been married some four months.

It was the end of Lon. In a rage he splintered his sluice box, broke his shovel and tore down the rough tent shelter. Lon set off downriver with murder in his heart. John Turner was the first man he saw.

"Howdy stranger," John called. "How about a cup of coffee? There's some left in the pot over by the tent and that fire can be stirred up in a minute. Help yourself. It sure is good country, isn't it? Been mighty good to me, anyway. How's your luck been?"

The question was the last asked by John Turner before Lon pulled the trigger. His body was found the following spring by a party of five miners who'd come over from the Feather River country to try their luck at mining on the Yuba.

"Must have been some kind of an accident," one of the men observed. "Looks like he might have been shot and then beat up some."

"Poor devil," called out another miner. "His luck was sure all bad. Here's his tent and there's not a sign of any gold dust. Diggings must not be too good up here, although that storekeeper down the river told us this was some of the best country in California.

"That Lon Crane may be a good storekeeper, but he sure don't know much about getting gold."

–June 4, 1964

MULE TRAIN TO RABBIT TOWN

Forty-five sturdy Mexican mules had started from Marysville, loaded with supplies that winter of 1852-53 for the Feather River mines. Before the journey was over their number would be thinned by a sudden, harsh, Sierra snowstorm.

Four Mexican muleteers kept a steady pace. One rode in front of the white bell mule and the others scattered through the single file of animals with one bringing up the rear.

They passed Brown's Valley on an overcast day, looking forward to clear skies of the higher elevations. At Brownsville the animals gave the sawmill an idle glance and kept slogging along the trail.

It was clear weather by the time the mule train reached Barker's Ranch or Barker's House as it was variously called. The community later came to be Woodville and today, Woodleaf.

At Strawberry Valley the muleteers gave their animals an extra day's rest to prepare for the climb up the ridge and down to Rabbit Town (La Porte). The men had no reason to hurry. There had been patches of snow visible on the high peaks, but days were warm and sunny.

The men started just before 9 a.m., the day after their rest. Each mule had waited by his own blanket and pack as the muleteers went down the line, blindfolding each animal, loading him, then removing the blindfold and moving to the next.

Several small ridges were crossed before they started the descent to Rabbit Town, and the men looked ahead and spotted Table Rock, covered with snow. It looked as if there were snow patches in the valley below, but it wasn't enough to cause alarm.

That night at near sunset the tired mules lined up, side by side, heads all turned the same way, as the muleteers started down the row, removing supplies and then aparajos, or pack saddles. An occasional animal kicked his heels as he scampered for the grass pasture. Others of a different turn, shivered pleasantly as would a woman who re-

moves her girdle for the day. They walked sedately to the pasture. The white mule's bell sounded more cheerful as he ended his day's work and pulled at the sweet grass.

The routine was repeated the next morning as the train left Rabbit Town for Little Grass Valley and then on to Onion Valley. The storm broke after they were through Grass Valley and winding their way along the South Fork of the Feather. Horizontal sheets of white blinded the leader, but he still had the creek to follow and was confident of his animals.

"Perhaps we wait it out here," he called to the second muleteer who rode up when the train halted. The animals were unloaded and grouped together. For three days snow fell as the men huddled together and mules stood against the storm. Sunshine broke through on the fourth day to reveal the pack train as an island in an ocean of white.

The only choice was to move to a lower elevation, back the way they had come. After losing four mules with packs it was decided to abandon the goods and try to save the animals. The men pulled, cursed and lashed, but there was only so much life and power, even in a sturdy, Mexican mule.

The animals plowed through chest high snow, struggled to the top of drifts and fell through to flounder. Many died trying to fight through. Many had to be abandoned where they stood. In all, the four numbed, ragged, weary muleteers stumbled back to Rabbit Town with three of their original 45 animals.

It was the beginning of one of the most severe winters of the Sierra. —JUNE 11, 1964

THE FRENCHMAN'S TRAVAILS

Many times during the early California gold rush, justice took a back seat and the "good guys" lost the fight to the bad. One such case occurred near the coastal camp of Trinidad, north of present-day Eureka.

A major character in the life and death drama was Alexander Andre who had come to California from Le Havre, France, in 1849. Word of the gold strike reached France in October, 1848, and several companies of Frenchmen formed with the purpose of sailing for California. It has been estimated that there were 20,000 French gold seekers here by March, 1852.

It took Andre's ship 181 days to reach San Francisco. He stayed but a short while in San Francisco, leaving there on April 13, 1850, for La Trinité (Trinidad). Ninety men were in the party which sailed from San Francisco on a 30-day cruise to La Trinité. Andre has explained that what should have been a two or three-day voyage took so much longer due to the quality of the ship, crew and captain.

Striking overland from La Trinité—the first town in Humboldt county to be settled by Americans—Andre and his group met a Spaniard traveling alone. The man told of meeting other Frenchmen on his way back from the mines and remarked with a sneer that one of the party had a fever and would probably be dead by the time they got to him. The Spaniard's appearance and manner bothered the Frenchmen and his words came back to them days later when they found the body of their countryman.

The man, described as being about 40 and fat, had been stabbed near the heart and dragged by a rope around his neck from a clearing to the forest. The Frenchmen buried him and agreed among themselves that the Spaniard must have been guilty. The dead man had been known to several of them and Andre remembered having sold the deceased a pair of shoes.

After an unsuccessful mine venture, the Frenchmen returned to La Trinité and informed the sheriff there, through an interpreter, of the dead man and their suspicions.

The sheriff had Indians on his mind and wanted to start a war against them. He attempted to get Andre and his friends to agree that Indians could have been responsible for the murder of the Frenchman. When the men stuck to their story, the sheriff appeared to lose interest.

Upon finding the Spaniard in La Trinité and wearing the dead man's shoes, Andre and his friends again sought the sheriff. They told their story over, adding what they felt to be their conclusive evidence, but the sheriff refused to arrest the Spaniard.

Four days later the accused man boarded the schooner Sierra Nevada and left the north coast a free man. The sheriff may not have wanted to become involved in any matter between foreigners, he may not have had a jail to hold the man or may have been too busy looking for Indian depredations to trouble himself. In any event, he shrugged off what appeared to Andre an obvious case.

Andre had found little to appeal to him in California. He noted that most American sailors and miners were drunk a great deal of the time and that Americans shot Indians as though they were animals.

The Frenchman left the Northern California coast for San Francisco and then home to France. He was gone, in all, just a little less than a year-and-a-half. He brought back no fortune, but was content that he escaped the wild frontier with his life.

–June 18, 1964

THE DUEL

Jim Denver had lived through the war with Mexico and never been called coward, but this morning as he checked the action of his rifle a feeling of doubt and unrest held him for a minute. There was something personal about a duel that made it so much different from any battle fought in a war between nations.

The date was August 2, 1852, and James William Denver had been challenged to a duel by ex-Congressman Edward Gilbert, a newspaper editor. They met at Oak Grove near Sacramento. The duel was to be fought with rifles at 40 paces.

Denver, a native of Frederick County, Virginia, had served as an officer in the war with Mexico. He had been a schoolteacher in Missouri and had graduated from Cincinnati School of law just before the war. Denver returned to Missouri after the Mexican war and then to California where he settled in Trinity County in 1850.

He was elected in 1852 to the state senate as Trinity county representative and because of this would face Gilbert over rifle sights.

Denver's difference with Gilbert resulted over the Emigrant Relief Train, a pioneer welfare-relief program authorized by the legislature.

Denver, in 1852, was named head of the relief train by Governor Bigler.

Gilbert, founder and editor of the *Alta California* in San Francisco, became dissatisfied with the relief train operation and charged both Denver and Governor Bigler with mismanagement. The charge could have been a true one or it could have arisen from personal feelings.

Following an exchange of verbal and printed insults, Gilbert challenged Denver to a duel. Frontier editors who were often called to back up what they had written were more commonly the challenged than challenger.

As Denver waited he shivered slightly in the chill, morning air. When the time came, seconds took the men's coats and they faced each other in the clearing. The grass was dew wet and the clear trail left by each could be easily traced.

At a signal there was a shot and, an instant later, another as Gilbert triggered his rifle in falling. James Denver stood for but a moment, looking on the man he had slain.

Gilbert was examined by an attending physician, pronounced dead, and his body lifted by seconds to a waiting wagon. There were no cheers. Men conversed briefly in muted tones and quietly left the grove.

Soon after the duel, Denver was appointed Secretary of State by Governor Bigler. Denver was elected to Congress in 1854 and three years later appointed commissioner of Indian affairs by President Buchanan.

He was sent to Kansas to make treaties with the Indians and then appointed governor of Kansas territory. While governor he announced his favor of the separation of Colorado territory from Kansas and is said to have suggested the name, "Colorado," for the new territory.

Despite his southern birth, Denver served as a brigadier general of Union volunteers in the Civil war, resigning in 1863 to return to law practice. He maintained a law practice until his death in Washington, D.C., on August 9, 1892.

While we look on James Denver as an adopted Californian who made good, Coloradoans thought even more of him. After becoming a territory their new capital was first named St. Charles and then changed to honor the man who helped make the territory possible.

–JUNE 25, 1964

GATEWAY TO THE FOOTHILLS

Shingle Springs on busy highway 50 in El Dorado county was a quiet way station on the road from Sacramento to Placerville in 1850. Mining brought some prosperity to the region, but a shingle mill and cool, refreshing springs were the town's main claims to fame and responsible for its naming.

The shingle mill was built in 1849 when the first big wave of migration swept over the Sierra. There was a need for shingles to roof the many cabins and stores in the foothills.

A hotel, the Shingle Springs House, was built in 1850 of lumber brought by ship around the Horn from the East Coast. Despite this sign of prosperity supplies still had to be purchased at Buckeye Flat, a mile to the east, until 1857 when Shingle Springs got its own store.

Four years later Planter's Hotel opened for business to accommodate

Sacramento Valley Railroad

the many travelers passing through on their way to or from the mountains.

The town boomed after 1865 when the Sacramento Valley Railroad extended its line from Latrobe to Shingle Springs. It became a center for teamsters who loaded wagons from the railroad cars. The route through Shingle Springs and Placerville was still the most popular one for east-bound freight at that time.

There was a decline two years later when Central Pacific finished its line through Auburn, diverting traffic to that route. With rail traffic available the cool springs offered less inducement for travelers planning a Sierra trip to pass through or to stop at the springs.

The community refused to completely die and was enough of a trade center in the 1880's that the Phelps store was built there. It was constructed of native stone with arched doorways on both first and second stories. Phelps built well with an eye for a steady stream of business in the years ahead.

Today, cars flash through Shingle Springs, their occupants intent on reaching the Sierra, Lake Tahoe or the gambling houses of Nevada.

On hot summer days it's easy to appreciate how pioneer travelers some 30 miles out of Sacramento on their way to the mountains, looked forward to a refreshing stop at the town with the cold well water.

A wagon driver might have planned the stop as a resting place after the second day's travel from Sacramento. A faster rider or hiker may have looked forward to reaching Shingle Springs in just one hot day and west-bound travelers surely lingered as long as possible before pushing on into the blazing heat of the parched, brown valley.

Shingle Springs has little to offer today's fast traveler who can leave the hot valley and be crossing cool, 7,000-foot Echo Summit in a few hours. It has little to offer except to serve as a reminder that many people passed this way and stopped before we became able to speed by. But then if we're to believe the modern slogan, "getting there is half the fun," perhaps we're the ones who have lost most by the decline of the many Shingle Springs.

–July 9, 1964

LAND SCURVY

Only the hardiest of the early gold seekers survived life in the gold camps, and it wasn't because of "shoot-outs," outlaws or other violence. There were those too, but the biggest killer was the food. During the first few years after the 1848 gold discovery there just wasn't enough fruit and vegetables in the camps.

Before the gold discovery there were many attempts to grow fruit and raise vegetables. Grains had been grown successfully and the beef supply was so large that carcasses were left to rot by ranchers who marketed only the hides.

With Marshall's discovery of gold every able man and boy left for the gold fields to make a fortune. Family gardens were neglected and the produce was left to rot in the ground.

The most severe nutritional disease was what has been called by some of the early miners "land scurvy." It was believed caused by exposure and the hard life miners lived in the wilds, as well as a salted meat diet.

Lacking a knowledge of vitamins, the miners were unaware that lack of vitamin C was responsible for their condition, but they were well aware that vegetables and "vegetable acids" were needed.

One miner, writing of his experience with scurvy, said many persons in his camp found they were unable to walk. There was a swelling and pains in their lower limbs. At first it was believed the condition was rheumatism, but scurvy was later settled on as the disease.

There was usually a swelling and bleeding of the gums as well as the swelling below the knees. The legs often turned black.

An afflicted miner who wrote of his condition said he was forced to continue his misery by eating more of the salted beef and pork in order to stay alive, but was also hurrying his own death. Incidentally, he paid $2 a pound for that beef and pork.

He was saved by a companion who found some sprouts which had possibly got their start in the wilds from the spilled beans of another pioneer. A boiled bean diet helped him recover enough to make his way into Coloma where he was able to buy potatoes at $3 a pound and live on them until completely recovered.

Another remedy for scurvy was to bury the patient in the ground with only his head showing. There are instances told of whole camps seeking the remedy at one time. A few able bodied men were stationed above ground to fend off the grizzlies and coyotes. We have never learned how effective the cure was, but it must have at least made burial of those who failed to recover easier.

A chance to make a fortune kept the miners in the mountains risking their lives and paying premium prices for whatever food was available.

Today, we have comfortable, warm sleeping bags, trailers and tents to make our mountain vacations comfortable. A wide choice of camping food is available at about the same prices paid in 1848 and 1849.

These men who were the first, have been said to have done work which included the talent and labor of canal building, ditching and masonry. They worked harder than needed to plow a field or to hoe potatoes. Their feet were usually wet all day long. They suffered the burning sun and cold, wet nights when a heavy dew made their meager blankets miserable. When we add the fact that the food they ate robbed them of as much strength as it gave, it's a wonder there were any survivors. —July 16, 1964

THE GENTLEMAN OUTLAW

Joaquin Murieta was a mystery during his brief, violent span of activity in California of the 1850's and has become even more of a mystery today. But then every Robin Hood has had the same problem of getting a decent biographer to handle his story.

There are several versions of his background and reasons for entering a criminal career. There is even a question about the length of that career although it appears to have been no more than two years and according to some historians even less.

We prefer the story of Joaquin as told by William James Howard, a member of the California Rangers, the group organized by the state legislature to track down Murieta's band.

Captain Howard said that Joaquin was born on a ranch in Sonora, Mexico. His parents were Basques, descendants of Murietas who had come from the Spanish Pyrennes to Mexico. Another version is that Joaquin came to California from Chile.

Joaquin was well educated, a sensitive youth who was adept on several stringed instruments and who loved dances and music.

When he was 17 he eloped with Rosita Feliz, a 16-year-old beauty whose father had a cabin on the Murieta ranch. The couple was married in Hermosillo and then left for California where Joaquin's half-brother, Jesus, told him a fortune was to be made mining gold.

The couple bought supplies in San Francisco and then made their way to the Stanislaus River country of the southern mines where they staked a claim.

Claim jumpers, finding the young Mexican at work, threatened him, telling him to leave the country. Spotting his beautiful, young bride, the men tied Joaquin and abused Rosita.

One story has it that Rosita or Carmela or Carmen as she was called by various writers, died as a result of the attack and Joaquin vowed vengeance. Captain Howard said that wasn't the case.

Rosita recovered and persuaded Joaquin to leave for Columbia to mine. There he was driven away by an anti-Mexican mob. At this stage it's easy to see how the young man was ready to be pushed over the edge and into all-out warfare against the American miners.

Howard said the final push came near Murphy's Diggings where Joaquin found a job as a monte dealer. Riding a horse loaned to him by his half-brother, Joaquin was stopped by a group of miners and accused of being a horse thief. Joaquin took the men to his brother who explained that he had bought the horse in good faith and had not stolen it. The accusers refused to listen.

Jesus was bound and hung. Joaquin was tied to a tree and lashed with a whip until his back was a bloody mass.

After the men left, the young Joaquin, who was then no more than 19 or 20, buried his brother and swore he would get revenge. He is said to have vowed that 20 men from Murphy's Diggings would pay with their lives for the loss of Jesus. He also swore that he would devote the rest of his life to killing Americans.

The vow is speculation, but Joaquin did leave the monte table and is said to have started his criminal career after Jesus's death. As a criminal Joaquin was always a gentleman with the lady prisoners and is said to have been popular with women of both high and low station. Most of his crimes were committed against Americans, but Mexican freighters suffered losses often attributed to Murieta.

–JULY 23, 1964

THE END OF JOAQUIN MURIETA

If only 60 per cent of local California legends are correct, Joaquin Murieta, the Robin Hood of the Sierra, spent more time in hiding than he ever spent robbing wagon trains or killing American miners.

From Shasta in the north to the Mexican border there are caves, rock outcroppings and other natural refuges where Joaquin is said to have hidden during his reign of terror or from either 1851 or 1852 until July 23, 1853.

It would have been impossible for Joaquin to have had as many different

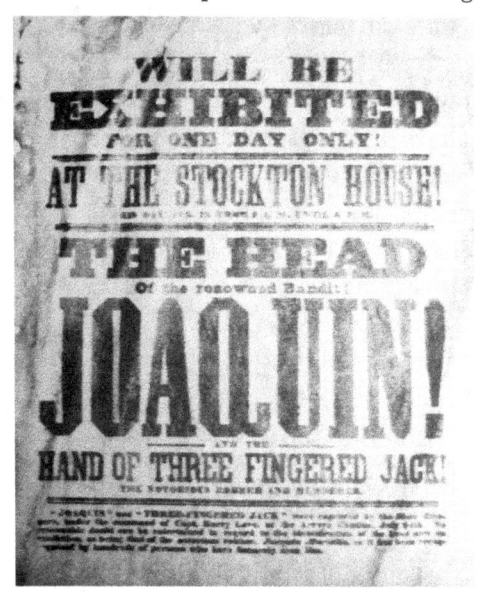

hiding places as have been attributed to him and still carried out any sort of self-respecting outlaw career. And yet there may be some truth in the legends.

Joaquin, a well educated Mexican who was greatly abused by American miners, set out on a criminal career to avenge the death of his half brother, Jesus. A natural leader, Joaquin collected a band of some 100 followers, all of them said to have been well mounted and well dressed. Each man carried an assortment of pistols and Bowie knives.

Reports of his widespread activities throughout most of the state become credible when we realize that Joaquin's forces were divided into five groups of roughly 20 men each. To confuse the issue, leaders of the separate bands were also named Joaquin. While Joaquin may have robbed a wagon train in Yuba County, another Joaquin could at the same time have held up a Southern California stage. Neither Joaquin may have been Murieta.

According to the longest surviving member of the California Rangers, William James Howard, Joaquin's various groups had headquarters near Marysville, Carillo Ranch, Mokelumne, Shasta and Cantura Canyon near the present town of Coalinga.

One of Murieta's most notorious men was Three-Fingered Jack who was killed by the Rangers with the real Murieta. Another member of the group was Reyes Feliz, a younger brother of Joaquin's wife, Rosita.

A friend of Joaquin's was Juanita, whose claim to fame rests on her accomplishment of having been the only woman hung in California. Juanita was strung up by an angry mob at Downieville, in 1851, when she killed an Australian miner who attempted to force his affections on her. Juanita is said to have believed that Joaquin would become strong enough to restore Mexican rule to California.

Loss of life and property to Joaquin's men became serious enough by December, 1852, that the state offered a reward of $3,000 for Joaquin, dead or alive. The following year, in May, 1853, the state assembly at Benicia authorized the governor to organize the California Rangers for the express purpose of ridding California of Murieta.

Captain Harry Love who headed the Rangers had been a scout, Indian fighter and a captain of spies in the Mexican war. Love selected 20 men, each with a reputation of self sufficiency and proven fighting ability, to staff the Rangers.

Each man carried full field provisions in the hunt for Joaquin. Wrapped in canvas and rolled in their blankets, tied to the back of each saddle, was a share of the group's food, a tin cup, tin plate, sugar spoon and individual coffee can.

Like Joaquin's men the Rangers carried Bowie knives and pistols. In addition, they packed rifles and shotguns and it was this added arsenal which is said to have brought Joaquin's career to an abrupt end when the two groups finally met in battle.

–JULY 30, 1964

The Daily Democrat is Yolo County's oldest continuously published daily newspaper. It is a newspaper of general circulation, providing full service news and sports information about Woodland and Yolo County government, businesses and individuals.

The paper was founded in 1857 and later owned by the Leake Family. It is presently owned by MediaNews Group, the second largest newspaper company in the United States.

www.ingramcontent.com/pod-product-compliance
Lightning Source LLC
Chambersburg PA
CBHW071529080526
44588CB00011B/1613